Outboard Boat
and Motor
Maintenance and
Repair

By Charles Dunne with Richard V. Nunn

GALAHAD BOOKS · NEW YORK CITY

Published by arrangement with Oxmoor House, Inc.
ISBN: 0-88365-340-0

Library of Congress Catalog Card Number: 75-32262

Manufactured in the United States of America

First Printing 1976

**Outboard Boat and Motor
Maintenance and Repair**

Editor: Candace C. Franklin
Cover Photograph: Taylor Lewis
Research and Photography: Mike Hilts

Acknowledgements

We gratefully acknowledge the
technical advice and photographic
assistance of the following: The Boating Industries Associations and the
Trailer Manufacturers Association,
both of Chicago, Illinois; the Aluminum
Association, Inc., New York; C & S
Engineering Co., St. Paul, Minnesota,
makers of Spartan Trailers, for help in
setting up the technical pictures in
Chapter Seven; Owens Corning
Fiberglas, Toledo, Ohio, for providing
the fiber glass repair photos in
Chapter Six; Mercury Marine, Fond du
Lac, Wisconsin, for help in setting up
many of the technical photographs in
the first three chapters; Johnson
Motors, Waukegan, Illinois, and
Evinrude Motors, Milwaukee, Wisconsin, division of Outboard Marine Cor-
poration, for photographic assistance;
and the Sailing Center of Chicago,
Oak Park, Illinois, for providing boats
and motors for photographic use.

Introduction
You own an outboard boat for fun and most likely for no other reason. Nearly everything else you own, including your car, was bought because you need it. But your boat is strictly for recreation, relaxation, and enjoyment.

And you want to keep it that way.

You want to spend every free hour on your boat—cruising, fishing, skin diving, water skiing. You certainly don't want to take on a new career—that of boat mechanic—but you should do a certain minimum amount of maintenance work on the boat. That is a normal part of being a skipper.

But when the work hours get too long and the fun hours too short, then owning a boat isn't fun anymore.

There are a couple of good reasons for doing some regular work on your boat. First of all, you want it to be dependable when you're out on the water. Good maintenance is the ounce of prevention which can help avert a breakdown in the middle of a lake or ten miles from shore in the ocean.

Secondly, good maintenance helps you get the service out of your rig that the manufacturer built into it. Outboard boats are built for long, de-pendable, and trouble-free service. The motors are compact giants, deli-vering a tremendous amount of horse-power per pound of engine weight—and doing so with great reliability for hours. But this reliability goes out the port hole if you have not done basic minimal chores such as tending to lubrication and tune-ups.

Finally, the well-maintained boat not only looks better and acts better while you own it—but it also is worth a lot more when the time comes to trade it in or sell it. The boat which has been given tender loving care always looks it and always commands top dollar.

Wait! That isn't the final value of good maintenance. The final value may be the embarrassment it will save. Suppose you invite the boss and his wife on an all-day cruise. Everyone makes the big effort and is on board bright and early eager for a day on the water. There is an air of expectancy as you slide into the seat behind the wheel and push the starter button. Nothing happens. You try a dozen more times and still the motor won't kick over. Your face gets redder and redder, and you produce a series of sputtering apologies. The last you see of the boss and his wife are their backs as they walk up the path away from the dock.

Do a decent job of maintenance and your baby will be shipshape and eager every time the weather is right. A good maintenance program, when organized properly, doesn't take a lot of time and won't cost you hours of fun. In fact, it will pay off in more hours of fun than it will cost.

Good Minimum Maintenance

What makes a boat fun?

That's easy. A boat is fun when she launches without grief, starts like a jack rabbit, runs for hours without a miss, handles easily in all kinds of water, doesn't guzzle you out of next month's mortgage payment, and generally behaves like the lady she was built to be.

She has to be dependable, easy to get along with, ready to go when you are, and cooperative even when the weather is not.

When she's new—fresh off the dealer's floor and all tuned up—a boat is all of these things and then some. There is no feeling quite like that of the first ride in a new boat when everything is in top shape and working at peak efficiency. You are flooded with feelings of pride and confidence.

But eventually time takes its toll. You get a scrape or two on the hull. You put a lot of hours on the motor and the timing gets a bit off. The spark plugs burn down a little and the prop chews through weeds and a few sandy bottoms. Someone spills soda pop next to the driver's seat; one of the running lights burns out; the rollers on your trailer become cranky.

That feeling of exhilaration disappears. The newness of the rig is gone, and you learn to live with less than full efficiency. In the beginning you could pull two water skiers easily, but now you have to bend the throttle to get them both up out of the water.

You have reached that point when maintenance is necessary. Everything mechanical gets to this point sooner or later, and under normal circumstances simple maintenance will restore the rig to like-new shape.

The sad fact is that if you don't do the maintenance—or have it done—the boat's performance will continue to deteriorate. There will inevitably come a time, probably a long way from shore or your home port, when the motor will heave a last sigh and sink into a coma. There is some kind of unwritten law which says that this will always happen when you least expect it or want it to happen.

One boater I know says he can always predict such breakdowns. They occur, he says, when he takes one last cruise before a tune-up, he's eight miles out, and a storm warning comes over the radio. He says his engine always conks out five minutes after he turns toward shore. One of his friends suggested that a sure cure for this situation is to turn the radio down so that the engine can't hear the storm warnings.

Maintenance of your boat, motor, and trailer is important and necessary, but it should not be a constant worry, cause a hassle, or subtract from the fun of owning a boat. If you do it right, you increase the dependability of the rig and invest no more than a few scattered hours. Most important of all, you regain that feeling of confidence you had when the boat was new just by knowing that everything has been tended to on schedule.

MAINTENANCE SCHEDULES

The first trick to keeping maintenance work to a minimum is to do the work on a regular schedule. The second trick is to keep a good record of what you do and when you do it. The third trick is one you borrow from airplane pilots: learn how to make

good, regular inspections of the boat, motor, and trailer.

From a maintenance standpoint you can divide each boating season into three parts:

Preseason: Get the whole rig ready for operation. This is the time of heaviest maintenance, and you should do the work in the weeks before you get into the water.

Midseason: Do what is necessary to keep everything running smoothly. During the boating season you want to spend a minimum of time on the shore and a maximum of time on the water.

Postseason: Take the rig out of the water and prepare it for winter storage. This is also the time to spend quite a few hours on maintenance work. What you do at this time has a

lot to do with how well the boat will run when you take it out of mothballs for the next season.

Obviously, you should set up time for heavy maintenance work in the pre- and postseason periods. If you do a lot of work at these times, you save on the number of hours you'll have to spend off the water during the season. The alternative is to do very little at the beginning of the season and scatter the rest of the work throughout the season. However, this method produces too many breakdowns and subtracts too many fun hours from good weekends.

Later chapters in this book will provide checklists and outlines of the necessary maintenance steps to take for your motor, boat, and trailer in each of the three seasonal periods.

RECORD KEEPING

Keep a record of everything you do to your rig. A one- or two-line entry in the maintenance log takes no more than five minutes each time you make a repair.

Establish a good maintenance record file in an expanding file envelope which is secured by an elastic band. In this envelope, keep, along with the maintenance log, the motor manual and instruction sheets which come with the different pieces of equipment you buy. This file provides one central storehouse of valuable information for work on the boat.

Buy three inexpensive notebooks; make one a log book for motor maintenance, another for hull maintenance, and the third for trailer maintenance. Or use one notebook divided into three sections.

Whenever you do any maintenance or repair work, always note the date and jot down a description of what work was done in the proper log. To be really thorough, note what parts you purchased along with part numbers and cost.

A quick review of these logs takes a minute or so and quickly tells you important things such as when the motor should be tuned again or how long it has been since you changed the lower unit lubrication. By being reminded of when each job was done, you know when it is due again—and can schedule the work before there is trouble.

As an additional precaution, add checklists of what should be done during the pre-, mid- and postseason. When you compare these to the log, you can see just what job is coming up next.

A maintenance envelope of this type can pay off in real dollars when you get ready to sell or trade in your boat. Simply show your records to the prospective buyer and tell him they come with the rig. He'll be able to see at a glance how well you've cared for the boat and will be delighted to get the manuals and records to help in his own maintenance work.

Keep a maintenance log for your motor, boat, and trailer in a record book. Store the log book and all important information sources such as operating manuals in a file envelope.

PROFESSIONAL HELP

Once upon a time the outboard motor was a cranky little one-lunger which was hard to start and even harder to keep going. The outboard owner could always be spotted around the boat club by the fact that he had grease under his fingernails and on his shirt front. He spent more time in the motor than behind it, and he had shoulder muscles well-developed from constant pulling of the starter rope.

One thing about those old motors: they were simple pieces of machinery, not very different from the motor on a today's lawn mower. After owning one for a season, you were qualified to take it apart and put it back together again. For the average boater motor repairs were a challenge, and you were not quite playing the game if you broke down and took your unit to the dealer for help.

Such days are gone forever!

Today's outboard motor is a marvel of engineering efficiency. The horsepower delivered by one engine not much bigger than a breadbox may be as high as 175. It is a high-compression masterpiece with the sophistication of a jet aircraft engine. It squeezes every ounce of power out of the fuel and drives more weight faster than could have been dreamed of as recently as 10 or 15 years ago.

The point is, the inside of a sophisticated engine like this is no place for an innocent, but well-intended, shade-tree mechanic. There are some things you can and should do about outboard motor maintenance, but there are a heck of a lot more things you should not attempt to do on your own.

Every marine dealer has looked up from his desk at one time or another to find a guy with a silly grin and a box full of parts. The story is always the same: he didn't think there was anything seriously wrong, so he decided to dismantle the motor himself. Would the dealer mind getting his mechanic to put it back together

again?

To avoid becoming the sad-faced guy with a box full of motor parts under his arm, decide right now to learn which repairs you are capable of and which ones are beyond you. Unless you are able to tear down and reassemble a current automobile engine, don't try taking your outboard motor apart.

How much professional help do you need in maintenance? And how much should you do yourself?

It depends on you: how talented you are mechanically, how much desire you have to putter around the boat, and whether you want to spend money rather than time. There are some jobs you *should not* try unless you are a first-class mechanic simply because they require special tools, special training, and experience.

There is another class of work you *could* do if you took a little time to learn how. For instance, tuning the engine requires know-how and some special tools, but it is a job which you might enjoy. One caution here: don't try jobs like this without a little education. Your outboard motor is too complex and too expensive a piece of machinery to use either for experimentation or as a learning device.

Finally, there is a good bit of work which you *should* do on your own. This includes items like cleaning the interior, washing and waxing the hull, and polishing the metal fittings. Of course, you could have everything done for you, but most outboard skippers feel better when they do some work themselves.

Jobs for the professional include any engine problems which require tearing down the motor; water pump problems; a bent propeller shaft; damage to the gears in the lower unit; any warping or twisting of the hull; most radio and electronics problems. It is a good idea to refer your motor to a pro for its annual tune-up because he can time the unit, adjust the carburetor, replace points, and do the other things

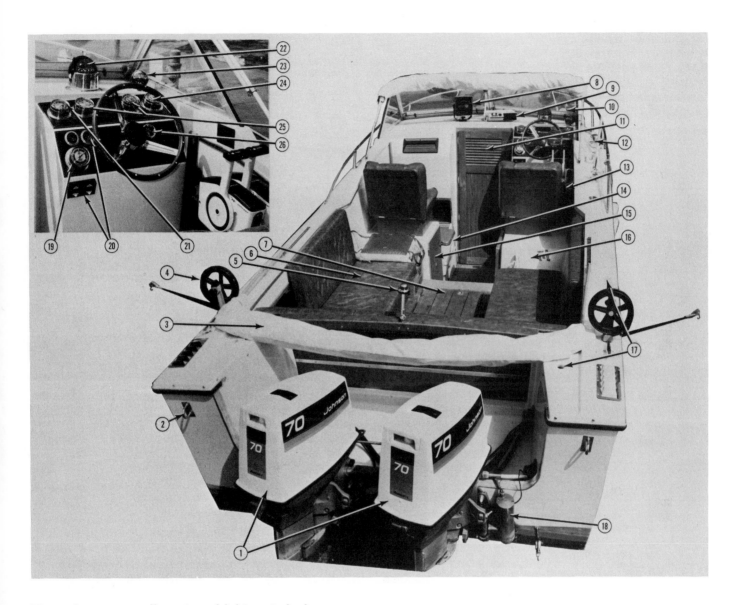

This is the way a well-equipped fishing rig looks.

1. Twin outboards
2. Lifting eye
3. Camper top
4. Downrigger
5. Running light
6. Folding seat/bed
7. Folding table
8. Sounder/locator
9. FM marine radio
10. Horn
11. Door to cabin with two beds, head, and storage
12. Search light
13. CB radio
14. Cooler
15. Sink and water supply
16. Refrigerator
17. Rod holders
18. Power trim and tilt
19. Barometer
20. Trim and tilt indicators
21. Marine clock
22. Compass
23. Motor synchronizer
24. Speedometer
25. Tachometer
26. Fuel gauge

For professional help, select a well-equipped marina and get to know the people there. Regular customers get preferred treatment, which can be important when you want work done quickly.

which can be tricky if you aren't an experienced mechanic.

Serious hull damage is a job for a professional. You can caulk your wooden hull when it is needed, and sand and paint your fiber glass hull. You can also fix minor leaks. But when it comes to replacing boards in the hull which have developed dry rot and making other repairs of that nature, let a good hull man do them for you. In the long run, it will be cheaper than doing it yourself.

The electrical wiring on small boats isn't too complicated, so with a little study you could handle any rewiring. The same is true of small trailers. But when you get to the bigger boats with plenty of electrical gears, the wiring becomes complicated—and a mistake can cost you some good equipment.

One thing you probably have

discovered already is that it pays to establish a good business relationship with one marine dealer. Buy your parts and materials from him and have him do your work. If you store your boat away from home, give the job to him. Most dealers will do whatever work a transient customer orders when he comes in, but the best service goes to regular customers.

BASIC TOOLS, PARTS, AND MATERIALS

You need tools to perform the maintenance on your boat—not many tools, fortunately, but sooner or later you will probably have some trouble while you are out on the water, and you'll need tools, materials, and spare parts to make quick repairs.

Space is at a premium in your boat, so obviously you don't want to fill it with large tool boxes which take up a lot of floor space and usually bark the shins of anyone walking past. For this reason, you might want to consider two or three small tool boxes, which can be conveniently stored in out-of-the-way places.

A tool collection is almost as personal as a shirt or pair of pants. It has to fit the user and his needs. One boater is more experienced at making basic repairs than another boater. One is good at setting up jury rigs with baling wire and chewing gum when things go wrong, while the next guy can do no more than pull out the oars and start rowing.

Tools aren't the only emergency equipment to carry. You'll need a small collection of spare parts, too. Consider both of the following lists as suggestions only. If you are very mechanically inclined, you may find the list of basic tools to be simple and incomplete. If you are the proud owner of ten thumbs, the lists may look complicated.

SPARE PARTS AND MATERIALS
  Cable for trailer winch
  Can of penetrating oil
  Cotter pins
  Electrical fuses in sizes needed
  Fuel filter element
  Light bulbs for each light on
    boat
  Light bulbs for each light on
    trailer
  Propeller
  Rags
  Roll of masking tape
  Roll of plastic electrical tape
  Sandpaper
  Small roll of flexible baling wire
  Spark plugs
  Starting rope
  Trailer wheel bearings
  Tube of all-purpose glue
  Tube of lower unit lubricant
  Tube of silicon gasket cement

BASIC OUTBOARD TOOL KIT
  Battery post cleaner
  Can opener (beer can type)
  File, small rattail
  Funnel, small
  Hacksaw, small
  Jack to raise trailer
  Knife (a good pen knife)
  Knife (type with replaceable
    razor-edge blades)
  Lug wrench for trailer wheels
  Oil can with spout
  Pliers, needle-nosed
  Pliers, regular
  Screwdrivers, flat bladed,
    several sizes
  Screwdrivers, Phillips, several
    sizes
  Set of Allen wrenches
  Spark plug gap gauge
  Wrench, large adjustable
  Wrench, socket, ⅜-inch drive
    with assortment of sockets
  Wrench, spark plug

If you are the type of boater who keeps his rig on a trailer and travels to different boating areas, the driveway, garage, or backyard are the best places to do most of your maintenance work.

If you have a house near the water, whether for summer enjoyment or year-round living, you can do much of the work at your own dock. To facilitate matters, it's a good idea to have a reliable boat-lifting winch to take the boat out of the water.

You should not expect to do your maintenance at your dealer's. This is a serious imposition unless he has made special space available for do-it-yourselfers. Some dealers have done this, but if 25 or 30 boaters turn out on a Saturday morning to paint their boats, the dealer won't have room to carry on his normal business.

Hull repair work is the messiest and requires the most space and preparation. Normal motor maintenance can be done with the motor on the boat and with the boat on the trailer or in the water. Trailer maintenance work can be done in your driveway.

When you head out on a vacation trip, have all the necessary maintenance work completed. Then you can drop in at lakes along the way without a care in the world.

The ship's store at your local marina is like a candy store full of tempting goodies. Browse around in it once in a while to spot new products and technical advances in equipment. Research keeps producing new and better things which make maintenance jobs easier.

Some parts of the maintenance operation are a family job, and everyone can help.

A few minor adjustments you should make on your motor and the lubrication of linkage assemblies and replacement of filters all can be done with the hood off right where you store the boat.

Preseason Motor Maintenance

In climates where you don't have the advantage of year-round boating weather, take your boat out of mothballs in the spring. By mid-February you probably begin to feel that itch and you know it's nearly time to get the boat out on the water. Since you can't break through the ice to launch, the best way to scratch that itchy feeling is to start on your spring boat work.

Visit your marine dealer and pick up any necessary supplies. This trip in itself serves as a kind of spring tonic. Check your maintenance records and plan your work. By the time the weather softens, you should be able to get out into the yard or driveway and get rolling.

If there is no winter to interfere with boating in your area, spring is a good time to declare a boating holiday: pull your rig out of service for a few days and give it a thorough going-over. Every boat needs an annual checkup.

To get your spring overhaul under way, make a complete inspection. If the boat was stored for the winter and your maintenance records or memory is good, you'll know what you did before you put her away, and this will help in the planning.

Go over everything with a magnifying glass. Look for such things as chipped paint, metal fittings that are loose, hull problems such as dry rot, barnacles which have adhered to the hull, and lines (ropes) that are frayed. Somehow, once the boating season gets under way, it is hard to find time for either a detailed inspection or for the nitty-gritty work that should be done.

DEALER-STORED BOATS

If you had the motor stored at your marine dealer, drop by and tell him when you expect to be ready for the water. His crew probably works on a fairly tight schedule at this time of the year trying to get all the boats and motors ready, so if you want your boat by a certain time, tell him, so that he can schedule it. Otherwise you'll take your turn.

While you are at the dealer's, talk over a few things with him. For example, is your battery good for another year? Probably. But if it is more than two years old, check it carefully. A lot of your boating fun depends on a healthy battery—one that is able to take a good charge and hold it. If you have any doubts, invest in a new battery. Like anything else, when your battery dies, it will do so at an awkward moment. You will save both grief and money by getting a new one before the old one forces your hand.

This is a good time to look at the propeller, too. If you gave it a beating last year so that it is full of nicks, think about getting a new one. Little edge nicks aren't serious and just need to be smoothed out. But big nicks—ones that have changed the contour of the blade even a little—can cause vibration, especially at high speeds. This vibration can damage the motor.

If there is hull work to be done, you should have told your marine dealer about it last fall so that the work could have been done over the winter. But it may not be too late even now. You may want the hull cleaned or painted, or you may need to have some of the fittings replaced. If you have a hankering for some new gear, such as a new ladder, this is a good time to order it and have it installed.

DRIVEWAY-STORED BOATS

If you have stored your boat, motor, and trailer in the driveway or garage, the entire inspection and maintenance job is up to you.

You have some alternatives: you can

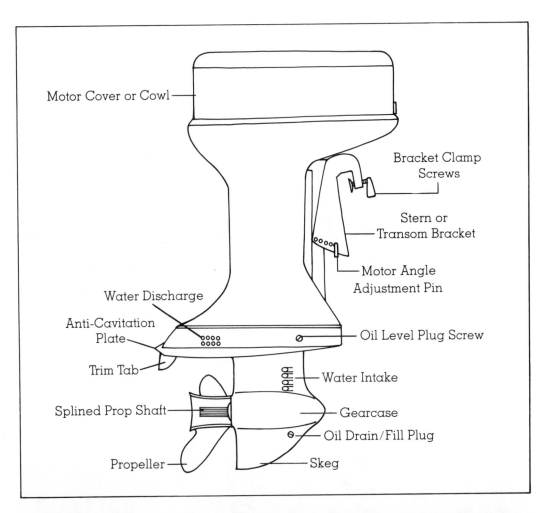

Motor Cover or Cowl

Bracket Clamp Screws

Stern or Transom Bracket

Motor Angle Adjustment Pin

Water Discharge

Anti-Cavitation Plate

Oil Level Plug Screw

Trim Tab

Water Intake

Splined Prop Shaft

Gearcase

Oil Drain/Fill Plug

Propeller

Skeg

do all the spring maintenance work yourself; you can do everything but the motor work yourself and then take the boat to your marine dealer; or you can simply hitch up and take the entire rig to him. Remember, however, that this is the busiest time of the year for the dealer. His first priority is given to people who stored their boats in his sheds over the winter; if you've stored your boat in your own garage, you'll have to make an appointment to get any work done, and you may have to wait a bit. A good time to see your dealer about this is in January before schedules get too hectic.

DO IT YOURSELF

If you have chosen to do the work yourself, concentrate on the items enumerated on the following checklist. Each item is accompanied by instructions for handling the maintenance work.

- *Remove cowl and clean motor.* The amount of cleaning you do

depends on what was done in the fall. If the motor was cleaned then, all you need to do now is spray everything under the cowl with anti-corrosive spray which is available at your marine dealer.

If it has not been cleaned in some time, you want to get all the oil and carbon and dirt off. Spray it with an emulsifying liquid such as Gunk, and let it sit for a while as directed on the can. Emulsifying liquid turns oily substances into a soapy, water-soluble material; when it has done its work, rinse away all the black "goop" with a garden hose.

Rinse with care and don't let water or any of the dirt get into the carburetor ports. Cover them with tape as a precaution. After rinsing, be sure all water is out of the motor compartment. Let the motor dry. Then spray it with an anti-corrosive.

Begin your preseason maintenance by conducting a thorough inspection of the boat, motor, and trailer. There shouldn't be very much work to do if you did a complete job of mothballing the rig last fall. Begin by cleaning the motor if it needs it.

• *Remove and check the spark plugs.* First remove the spark plug cables by grasping the metal fitting or housing on the plug with your fingers (do not grasp the wire); then pull the cable off the plug. Remember that the wires must go back on the same plugs. If you put them on different plugs, you'll create problems. You should be able to tell which wire goes to which plug by the length of each wire and the way it is laid out into the motor. If you have doubts, remove and replace only one plug at a time.

Use a spark plug wrench and proceed with care. Your motor has an aluminum head into which the spark plugs are fitted. Aluminum is relatively soft and easily damaged. If the plug sticks, a sharp blow on the wrench with the heel of your hand will generally loosen it—after which it should turn easily.

Remove all the plugs and inspect them. Do the electrodes appear burned away, or are they covered with a deposit? If they look good, you can clean them and use them again. Some service stations have spark plug cleaners and will clean them for a fee. Or you can scrape them with a sharp knife, cutting away all deposits from the electrodes and from the ceramic portion of the plugs.

Many boaters prefer not to use old plugs and always start each boating season off with new plugs. Sound reasoning supports this practice: you save the cost of new plugs by using old ones, but by installing new plugs you may gain the advantages of lower fuel consumption, easier starting, and smoother running. The biggest point in favor of new plugs is that the new ones will be more dependable.

Whether you use old or new plugs, you *must* adjust the spark gap before you install them. Check your motor manual to determine the correct spark gap. If you don't already have one, buy an inexpensive spark plug gapping tool.

Set the gap by bending the electrode arm slightly toward the center of the plug; then run the correct feeler or arm on the gapping tool between the center electrode and the electrode arm. The feeler or arm of the gapping tool should pass through the opening with some pressure. If it passes through too easily, the gap is too wide and the electrode arm must be bent a bit more.

Some motors have a different kind of spark plug, one of surface gap design. These plugs don't have the familiar bent-over electrode arm. Instead, they have only a slender metal electrode protruding from the center of the base. These plugs don't need regapping because there is nothing to gap. They have an exceptionally long life, but must be changed occasionally. Do not replace regular spark plugs with surface gap plugs in your motor. The two plug types are *not* interchangeable.

Inspect surface gap plugs for badly worn electrodes and for glazed, broken, blistered, or lead-fouled insulators. If the center electrode is burned back 1/32 inch or more below the insulator, the plug should be replaced.

Always replace all the spark plugs in your motor at the same time, not just one now and another next month. Buy the plugs in sets of the same make and type number. Be sure to get exactly the same type of plug you already have; spark plugs are not freely interchangeable. The heat range, for example, is controlled by the length of the plug base. A change

Use a spark plug wrench or other wrench of the proper size to remove the spark plugs. Remember that the aluminum head of the motor is easily damaged. When removing and reinstalling spark plugs, proceed with care. When installing the plugs, be sure each plug turns easily into its hole. If it sticks, do not force it to turn or you may strip the threads; remove the plug, apply a drop of motor oil to the threads, and try again—gently.

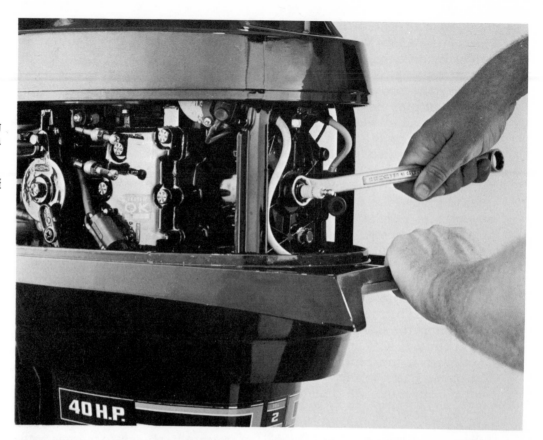

After cleaning old spark plugs, or when installing new plugs, you must first gap them. Use a gapping tool for the job. Review your motor manual to learn what the correct gap should be; then select the corresponding wire loop or feeler on the tool. (Numbers are stamped on the side of the tool.) Pass the wire between the electrodes as shown. It should pass through with a little pressure. If it passes through too easily, bend the electrode arm slightly toward the center electrode and try the gapping tool again.

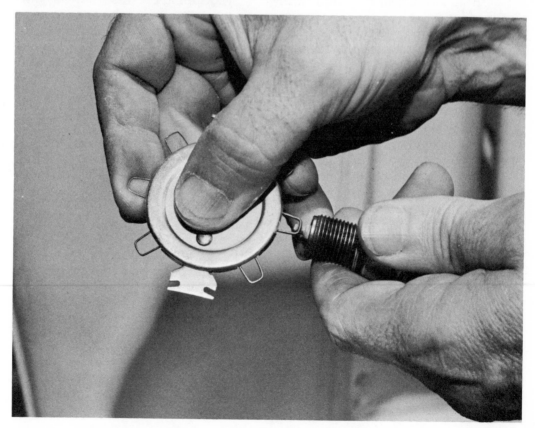

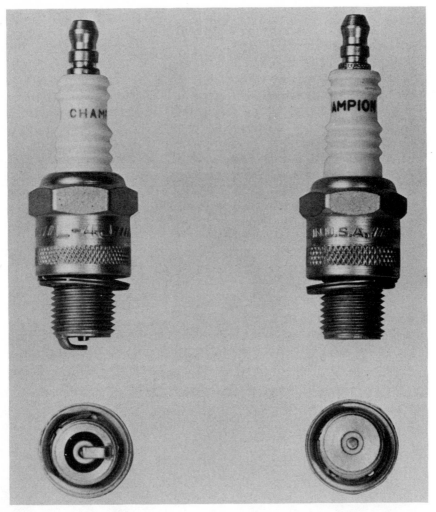

The spark plug on the left is the standard design used in gasoline engines for many years. The one on the right is the new "surface gap" plug. If your motor requires plugs of the surface gap type, they do not need regapping and have a very long life but must be changed occasionally.

in spark plug types may make a big difference in the way your motor runs; most of the time, the change is probably for the worse.

If you suspect that you need a different type of plug—if your motor misses or the plugs become fouled too frequently—talk with your dealer's mechanic. He can recommend a hotter or colder running plug. But your best bet is to stay with the manufacturer's recommendations which you'll find in the manual.

Each spark plug is seated on a metal gasket. The gasket is a hollow copper ring, and when you install a new plug, put the gasket over the base before threading the plug into its port. As you tighten the plug down, the gasket is compressed to make a gas-tight seal and a good heat contact.

When you remove a plug, the gasket will stay compressed. If you decide to use the old plugs, use new gaskets, which can be hard to find. Your dealer may have them but make sure what he has is the right size for your plugs. Most of the time, the only place you'll see a new gasket is in the package with a new spark plug. So you may have to reuse the old gasket.

The professional mechanic uses a torque wrench with a gauge on it to install spark plugs. The plug manufacturer specifies how many pounds of torque pressure should be applied to properly tighten the plug. The mechanic first turns the plug into the port finger-tight; then he applies the wrench and gives it the correct pressure.

If you don't have a professional torque wrench, tighten the plug finger-tight, then apply a regular plug wrench and give it about a quarter turn. This will approximate the specified pressure. Note that this is for installing a plug with a new gasket. If you are using the old gasket, which is already compressed, use less than a quarter of a turn—just enough to tighten the plug so vibration won't loosen it.

Be extremely careful when threading spark plugs, old or new, into your motor. They should thread in easily. Never force a plug that sticks as you turn it. Instead, turn it back out and start over. By force-turning a plug, you may foul up the threads in the plug port. This can be an expensive mistake since once the threads are crossed by forcing in this manner, you'll never be able to seat a plug properly again. The remedy is to buy a new head for your motor. Force-turning a plug is one of the most common goof-ups scored by do-it-yourselfers.

- *Lubricate under the hood.* When the spark plugs have been replaced, check your motor manual to find out what needs lubrication under the hood. Every motor is a little different in this respect. The manufacturer's manual will tell you what kind of grease or oil to use, and you can buy the right kind in tubes from your dealer. Generally speaking, you should lubricate the various linkages.

While the hood of the motor is off, lubricate each of the linkage points using a heavy grease which is available in tubes from your marine dealer.

• *Check fuel lines and fuel fittings.* They should fit snugly and show no signs of damage. If the lines look worn or chewed, and if the fittings are tight, get new lines. They come ready-made at your dealer's, with fittings and hose cut to size for your model.

Every motor has a fuel filter in the fuel line near the carburetor. Some are easy to get at, and some are just plain devils. In most recent motor models manufacturers have tried to make the filters more accessible. Check the manual for the location of the filter on your motor.

The manual will caution you to disconnect the fuel line plug-in connector before taking the fuel filter apart to prevent spilling fuel. In this spring maintenance, the fuel line should be disconnected before you begin. If it isn't, unplug it now.

Use a screwdriver to loosen the screw on the fuel filter. Every manufacturer uses a different filter design, but it is basically a bowl or similar container, in which the filter element rests. Use fresh gasoline as a solvent to clean the element. If you can't get it clean, then install a new element. Clean the filter bowl as well; then reassemble the filter.

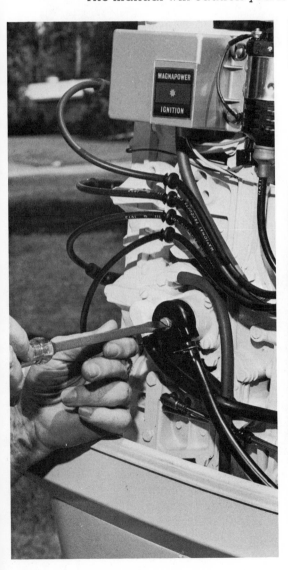

Every motor has a fuel filter in the fuel line near the carburetor. The filter element should be checked and cleaned, not only during preseason maintenance but also during the boating season. In the Chrysler motor at left, the filter is low on the right side. In the right-hand photo of a Mercury motor, the filter is high on the right side under the flywheel. In both cases, opening the filter is easily done with a screwdriver.

After the cover of the fuel filter has been removed, the filter element comes right out. Normally all that is necessary is a simple cleaning with gasoline; then the element can be reinstalled. Filter elements rarely need to be replaced.

It is vital to good operation to drain and change the lubricant in the lower unit regularly. You should do so when putting the motor into storage and again before starting the motor in the spring. To drain the unit, put the motor in the upright position with a pan under it. Remove the drain plug (in the grease filler hole) and loosen or remove the vent screw. Give the lubricant time to drain. To fill the unit with fresh lubricant, fit a tube of lower-unit lubricant into the filler hole and squeeze the tube until lubricant begins to ooze out of the vent opening. Replace and tighten the vent screw; then take the tube of lubricant out of the filler hole. With the vent screw tight, lubricant will not run out of the unit. Now install the plug in the filler hole.

Before replacing the vent screw and drain plug, make certain the gaskets under the screw heads are in place. Otherwise, water could leak past the threads and into the gear housing.

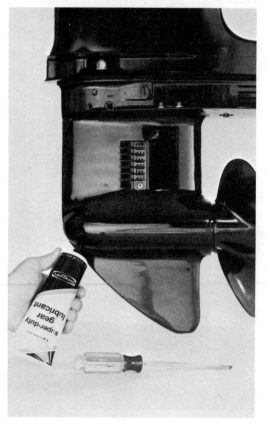

- *Drain and refill lower unit of motor.* There are two screw plugs, one above the other, on the vertical part of most lower units. The upper one is the vent screw; the lower one is the drain plug. To drain the unit, remove the drain plug and loosen or remove the vent screw, but don't do it until you have placed a pan or bucket under it to catch the old lubricant.

Allow enough time for all the lubricant to run out, and take a look at it as it gathers in the pan. If the old lubricant looks milky, it has emulsified with water which means that the lower unit probably has a leak. You need to have the gasket between the upper and lower unit replaced by a professional. To add new lubricant, fit the tube of lubricant to the drain or lower opening, and squeeze it until lubricant begins to ooze out of the upper opening. Now put both plugs back into their holes.

• *Check the propeller.* While you are working on the lower unit, take a look at the propeller. If it is chewed and nicked, it may give you trouble. If the nicks are small and appear only at the edges, use sandpaper or a file—gently—to smooth them out. If they are large, or if the contour of the blade is changed even a little bit because of them, the motor may vibrate when run. This is not only annoying and power-robbing, but it also can seriously damage motor parts. Install a new propeller.

When the motor was new, the dealer installed a propeller, following manufacturer's recommendations, which was right for the size of the boat and motor and the kind of use you expected to give it. If you have had satisfactory service from this propeller, then buy another just like it.

You can change your prop, however, if you want to change the way your boat behaves. The art of matching the propeller to the boat and the motor is complex and a number of factors must be considered. With the wrong prop, you can lose speed or pulling power and increase fuel consumption. The selection of a different prop from the type you have been using calls for a conference with the prop man at your marine dealer.

While you are checking the prop during spring inspection, take a moment to check the spare parts locker. Do you have a spare prop which you carry with you in the boat? You should have, because you never know when you may accidentally chew up a submerged log and ruin the prop on the motor. You can install a

At the start of the boating season, remove the propeller and coat the splined shaft with gasket sealing compound. To keep the prop gears watertight, repeat the procedure about every 60 days during the boating season and again when you put the motor away for the winter. Each motor has a slightly different propeller assembly. In the Mercury motor pictured, first wedge a block of wood between the prop blade and the lower unit housing as shown. This serves two purposes: first, it prevents accidental starting of the motor, which can happen if you turn the prop when the motor is ready to run. When checking the propeller during the boating season, disconnect the battery before starting to work on the propeller. Secondly, the block of wood keeps you from cutting your hands on the edges of the propeller blade. After the propeller blade has been secured, use a wrench to loosen the large nut which holds the propeller on.

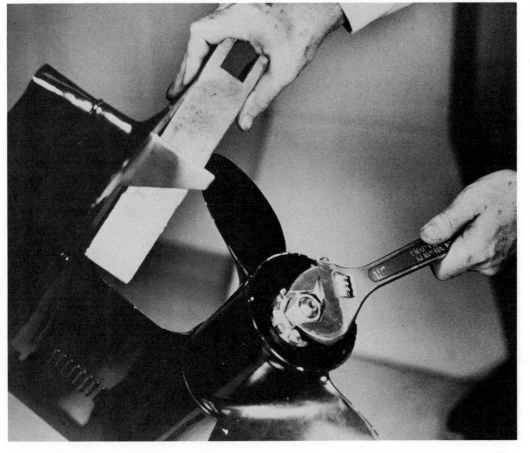

With the large nut loose, lift the tabs of the tabbed washer. (In other motor styles, a cotter pin replaces the tabbed washer.) The tool in the picture is a specially-made pair of pliers available at your marine dealer's; it is inexpensive and does the job quickly. Normally, three tabs of the tabbed washer have been bent down, and three have been bent up.

With all the tabs bent up, use a screwdriver and hammer as shown to tap the large inner nut loose. Two or three light taps with the hammer will usually do the job. Next turn the nuts off the shaft and pull the propeller off. Sometimes getting the prop free takes a pretty good pull, and there are tools called prop pullers to help. But most of the time, it will come free without any special tools.

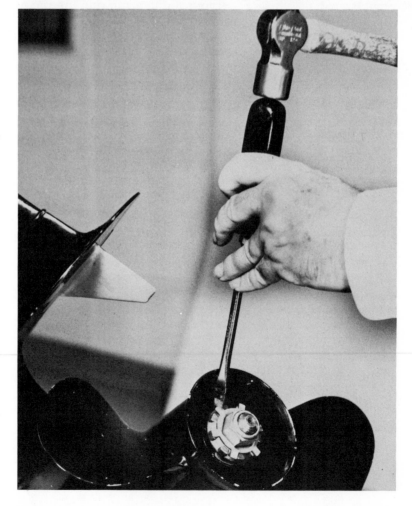

With the propeller off the shaft, apply a generous coat of gasket sealing compound to the shaft. You can buy the sealing compound under different names at your dealer's. After applying the sealing compound, slip the propeller back on the shaft and reverse the disassembly procedure: replace the largest nut and tighten it with a couple of light taps with the hammer and screwdriver. Put the tabbed washer on and bend three tabs down as far as you can. Then reinstall the final nut and tighten with a wrench.

new prop on the scene without much difficulty as long as the propeller shaft has not been bent. If it is bent, row ashore and pay a visit to a mechanic.

Changing a propeller is an easy job. You need only two tools, and the whole process should not take more than five minutes. Since you may change propellers frequently, you might as well make the job easy by buying the right tools—in this case, a wrench to fit the prop nut. A ratchet wrench with a socket sized to fit the nut is a good investment. First, loosen the large nut which holds the propeller in place. Next, you will need a pair of pliers to remove and reinstall the cotter pin. If you have a Mercury motor, the prop assembly is slightly different and a tabbed washer is used instead of a cotter pin. To remove the splined washer, you will need an

inexpensive tool which looks like a pair of pliers, but has its jaws shaped to bend the tabs on this washer with ease.

For Johnson, Evinrude, and most other motors follow this step-by-step procedure: remove the cotter pin on the end of the propeller shaft; loosen and remove the propeller nut; take the spacer off the shaft; and remove the propeller. To install a propeller, first coat the splined shaft with gasket sealing compound, slip the propeller on the shaft, and then reverse the previous procedure, completing the job by installing the cotter pin in the propeller shaft.

The procedure is a little different for Mercury motors. First remove the propeller nut; bend up the tabs on the tab washer and remove it; use a screwdriver to tap the splined washer loose and remove it; then remove the propeller. To install the new prop, coat the prop shaft with gasket cement, slide the new prop on, and reverse the removal procedure.

You should include a block of wood among your propeller tools. When you are working on it, the propeller turns freely; thus it can be hard to handle and may cut your hands. If you wedge the block of wood between one blade of the propeller and the anti-cavitation plate (just above the propeller on the lower unit), it will hold the propeller while you work on it.

WARNING. If the fuel lines and battery are connected, it is possible to start the motor by turning the propeller. *Never* work on a propeller without taking the proper precautions to prevent accidental starting. Check your manual.

Mercury tells you to turn the key switch to the OFF position, and to place a block of wood between the prop blade and the anti-cavitation plate. Johnson, Evinrude, and other motor manuals tell you to shift the throttle-shift lever to the NEUTRAL position, and to disconnect the spark plug leads.

Pay serious attention to these instructions. You could be severely injured if the motor started while you were working on it.

• *Replace the cowl, and check motor for nicks or scratches;* use touch-up paint to cover them. You can then give the motor a coat of wax to improve appearance and for protection.

• *Lubricate or oil exterior motor fittings.* These include such items as clamp screws, reverse lock levers, and the swivel brackets. Each make and model is different, so check the manufacturer's manual to learn which items to lubricate, where to apply the lubrication, and what lubricant to use.

• *Check fuel tank and fuel.* As a

Now lubricate all the exterior fittings of the motor. Check the manufacturer's operating manual to learn what needs to be lubricated and what type of lubricant to use. On this motor the tilting arms are lubricated with a simple grease gun which consists of a fitting attached to the tube of lubricant. Each make of motor differs in the type of lubricant recommended and the method of application.

general rule, you should not use old gasoline. After several months of storage it gets gummy. If you store gasoline over the winter, add the product Sta-Bil to it which stabilizes the fuel and prevents gumming. But the best bet is to use fresh fuel right from the beginning of the season. If there is stale fuel in your tank, get rid of it.

If you stored your tank dry, or if you think it needs cleaning, slosh a couple of quarts of fresh gasoline around in it, and discard the gas when finished. Examine the filter on the fuel pickup tube in the tank for dirt. Clean it by adding a little fresh gasoline and sloshing it back and forth for a few seconds. If the tank shows any signs of rust, sand the area to remove the rust; then apply touch-up paint.

• *Bring battery out of storage.* When carrying the battery, handle with care. Remember that the electrolyte in the battery is an acid which can burn your skin and cause serious injury to the eyes. If some of it should splash out of the battery onto you, wash the affected area immediately with water.

If you coated the battery terminals with grease last fall, wipe them clean with a cloth, leaving a thin film as protection. If you didn't clean and coat the terminals at the end of last season, get your trusty little battery post cleaner out and do it now. And while you are at it, use the wire brush part of the battery post cleaner to clean the battery lugs. Simply run the brush up and down through the lugs a few times.

The big question is, of course, whether or not the battery is charged sufficiently. If you have put it on the trickle charger inter-

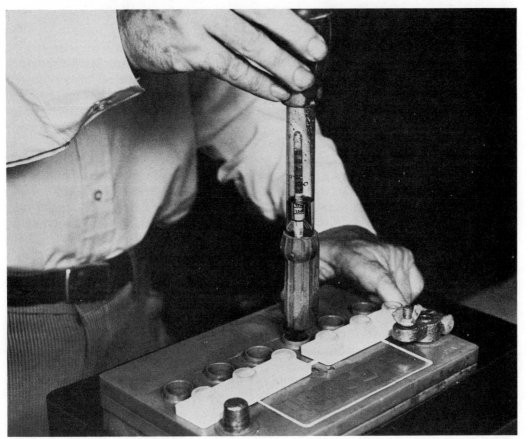

At the beginning of the boating season, check to see if your boat's battery is good. You can have any gasoline service station or your marine dealer check it with a hydrometer, or you can buy your own hydrometer for about $3. If the battery is fully charged, the hydrometer should read 1.260 specific gravity. If the reading is below 1.230, the battery should be charged. If a good charge doesn't bring the reading up to 1.260, the battery is probably nearing the time when it must be replaced.

Last fall you probably coated the battery posts with grease to protect them over the winter. During preseason maintenance, wipe the grease off, leaving a very light coat of film for protection. If, however, you have not cleaned the battery posts in some time, use a battery post cleaner—the kind you can buy in any automotive store. It is nothing more than a stiff wire brush built into a cap which fits over the battery post. As you turn it back and forth a few times, it cleans the post down to bare, bright metal.

mittently during the storage period, and especially for a day or so in the past week, it probably is ready—providing the plates are good.

If you have doubts about the ability of the battery to take and hold a charge, let your dealer check it cell by cell. Or, for about $3, you can buy a hydrometer and check it yourself. Testing all the cells takes only a few moments, and instructions come with the unit.

Put the battery in position on the boat, but don't make the connections until you are ready to start the motor. As a safety precaution, you should always disconnect the positive (+) battery cable when the boat is in transit or parked between trips. This eliminates the possibility of the motor accidentally starting.

You still have some preparatory work to do on your boat and trailer before heading for the water, but much of the preseason maintenance has been covered in this checklist. Later chapters will outline the final steps to take in getting your rig ready for a successful boating season.

Meanwhile, remember: *don't ever start your motor unless the lower unit is in water.* An outboard motor depends on water pumped in through ports in the lower unit for cooling; even a short burst of activity without this cooling water can seriously damage it.

Marine dealers often use tanks or barrels full of water for testing purposes. The motor is mounted on the side of the tank with the lower unit submerged in water. Unless you are prepared to set up such a test tank, don't try to start the motor until the boat is in the water.

Midseason Motor Maintenance

You've launched your boat with a nice splash, and the season is now officially under way. Your first chore is to get the motor started for the first time. After that, all you have to do is some simple maintenance and know what to look for in the event of unexpected trouble.

Before starting the motor for the first time, you should fill the fuel tank with fresh fuel, make all of the electrical connections on the boat except the battery cables, and finally connect the battery. Then you'll be ready to push the starter button.

FUEL MIXTURE

Don't begin the season with a tank of fuel left over from last year. As mentioned earlier, gasoline doesn't store well—it gets gummy after a few months. Fill your clean gas tank with new outboard oil and fresh fuel.

Most newer outboards use a fuel mixture of fifty parts gasoline to one part outboard oil. Recommended gasolines are the standard 89 octane in either regular or lead-free grades. Outboard oil comes packaged in pint cans, which you can buy individually, in six-packs, or by the case. Don't use regular automobile oil—only an oil specified for outboard motor use.

To fill your fuel tank, *first* pour in the required amount of oil. Then fill the tank with gasoline. Some manufacturers recommend that you mix the oil and fuel by putting the filler cap securely on the tank and then tipping the tank on its side and back to the upright position.

What happens if you use the wrong oil/fuel mixture? Well, if you use too little oil, you can damage the motor through lack of lubrication. If you use too much oil, you may get spark plug fouling, erratic carburetion, excessive smoking, and a quick build-up of carbon in the motor.

For quick reference, here is a table of the amount of oil required to make the correct mixture:

3 gallon tank . . . . .8 ounces
(½ pint) of oil
5 gallon tank . . . . .12 ounces
of oil
6 gallon tank . . . . .16 ounces
(1 pint) of oil

BATTERY CONNECTIONS

Now make all of the electrical connections in the boat except the battery. Turn the ignition switch to the OFF position. Plug the electrical harness into its receptacle on the motor. Be sure the remote control cables are connected.

Before you connect the battery cables, be aware of the fact that if you connect them improperly—that is, if you put the wrong cable on one of the battery posts—you will immediately damage the charger and other electrical components. This will cost you time and money—so pay attention to what you're doing.

First connect the red cable to the positive (+) terminal of the battery. Slip the terminal lug down over the post, and then tighten the nut on the lug until the lug is firmly in contact with the post. You should not be able to move the lug after the nut has been tightened. Next connect the black cable to the negative (–) terminal of the battery and tighten it into place. Coat both the positive and the negative connections with petroleum jelly or a heavy grease to protect them from corrosion.

MOTOR OPERATION

Before tilting the motor into the water to start it, make a visual check of the

Modern outboard motors operate on a mixture of oil and gasoline at a ratio of one part oil to fifty parts gasoline. Too much or too little oil in the mixture can cause operating problems. Take a moment to double check the amount of oil you are putting into the tank. Most gas tanks have labels with the correct mixing formula printed in plain sight. Always pour the oil in the tank first, followed by the gasoline.

Always remove the gas tank from the boat when filling it. One of the greatest sources of accidental boat fires is an accumulation of gasoline fumes on board the boat, usually in the bilges or in other confined areas. Gasoline fumes can be ignited by any spark—even the spark created when you turn the starter. To avoid spilling gasoline in the boat, put the tank to be filled on the dock; then cap it before lifting it back into the boat. If any gasoline has been spilled on the tank, wipe it off before putting the tank in the boat.

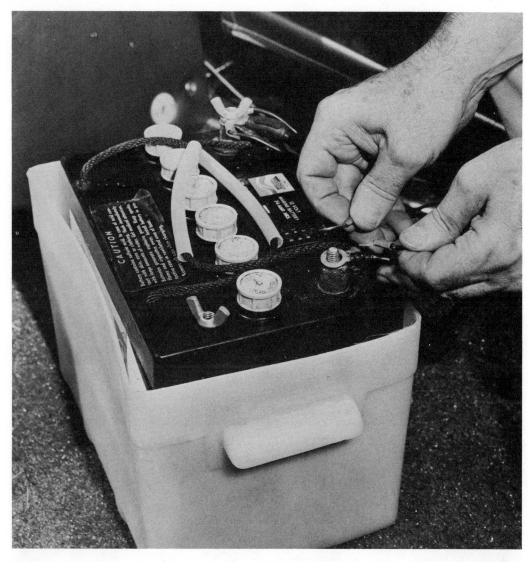

When the boat is ready for the water, reinstall the battery. Do the job carefully. Remember, if you connect the battery cables to the wrong posts, you will cause immediate and expensive damage to the charger and other electrical components. First connect the red cable to the positive (+) battery terminal. Slip the terminal lug down over the post; then tighten the nut which holds it. All the boat's instrumentation is connected directly to the battery, and so you may have several wires to connect to each battery terminal. Make sure those wires which belong on the positive terminal are connected to it. Next, connect the black cable and any corresponding instrument wires to the negative (–) battery terminal. When all connections have been tightened, coat the terminals with a light coat of protective grease or petroleum jelly.

water intake ports on the lower housing to see that nothing is blocking them. If all is clear, start the engine in the normal manner. Run the motor at reduced RPMs for a few minutes to allow it to warm up and to get rid of any oil accumulation which may have built up in it.

After starting the motor, make sure the water pump is operating. Remember, the motor depends on water pumped in through the lower unit for its cooling. If the pump isn't working, the motor will heat up quickly and could be severely damaged. Some motors have warning horns which sound when the engine overheats. If the horn sounds, shut off the motor immediately and check the water intake for a blockage. Don't attempt to run a motor which overheats, even at very reduced speeds. If the problem persists, see your mechanic.

If your motor runs smoothly after its warm-up, don't tamper with it. Just go out and enjoy the day.

If it doesn't seem to be running as well as it should, a simple adjustment of the idle screw may help. The idle screw may be in a different location on each motor, and each manufacturer recommends a slightly different method of adjustment. For specific details, check the manufacturer's operating manual.

Never start your motor unless the lower unit is in the water. Become familiar with the water intake parts on the lower unit: in this picture the port is the screened opening with the two vanes in it. Whenever you inspect your motor, look at the ports to be sure nothing—paper, seaweed, etc.—is blocking them. If you attempt to run the motor when the ports are blocked, it will receive no coolant and will be seriously damaged after a few minutes of operation. In the beginning of the boating season, when you start the motor for the first time, first tip the lower unit of the motor into the water, then start the motor. Be sure the water pump is working and the engine is being cooled.

You may have to adjust the idle screw if the motor doesn't run as smoothly as it should after it warms up the first time. You need only a screwdriver. Check your manual for the location of the idle screw and for the recommended method of adjusting it. In this photo, the idle screw is plainly visible—it is the screw with the spring around its shaft.

MAINTENANCE CHECKS

Once your boating season has started, you'd like to keep maintenance work at a minimum. If you anticipate what must be done and set up a schedule for the work, you can spread the work out so that it takes no more than 10 or 15 minutes on one day each week. The only exception to this is the motor tune-up.

If you prefer to lump most of your maintenance work into one period in the middle of the season, you can do so. Just plan to take the boat out of service for a few days.

To stay in top shape, your motor should have a tune-up and have thorough maintenance service after each 50 hours of operation. When the maintenance schedule calls for lubrication every 60 days, it assumes the normal hours of operation by the average boat owner. The average boat owner probably doesn't *run* his craft more than 10 or 12 hours a week—though he may spend much more time than that on board.

It might surprise you to learn how many hours of actual operating time you put on your motor. As an experiment, keep a card beside the driver's seat, and log the actual hours and minutes when the motor is running. Do this for a couple of weeks and you'll be much sharper at estimating when maintenance is necessary.

Look over these maintenance chores at the beginning of the boating season and schedule the weekends when you will do them in advance. The real purpose of such advance scheduling is to remind you to do what must be done. If you find you are running the boat more than usual, you might move the schedule up a week or two.

During the boating season, schedule maintenance time for the following items:

- *Have a complete professional tune-up once during the season.*

You can do many maintenance chores right in your driveway, but there are three things you should not do. First, do not connect the battery until you get the boat to the water. Second, do not fill the fuel tank until you are near the water, since towing a boat with full fuel tanks is asking for trouble in the event of an accident. Third, do not start the motor in the driveway; wait until the boat and the motor's lower unit are in the water.

Before tipping the motor into the water, go over all the wiring, especially if you did not do so during preseason maintenance. Check to see that all wires are tightly connected and that none of the connections are corroded. Clean and tighten where necessary. A loose or dirty connection can play havoc with the boat's operation and can sometimes be extremely difficult to locate.

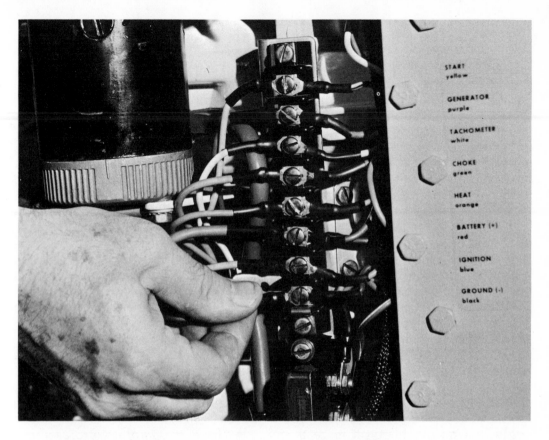

After all, you have a hefty investment in this power plant, and you want to get the most out of it. Of course, if you have the tools and equipment and understand what you're doing, you can tune it yourself.

If you want the job done for you, make an appointment with your marine dealer and plan to leave the boat with him for a few days. When the job is finished, find out if new breaker points, spark plugs, or other parts were installed, and note the replacements in your maintenance log.

- *Check the propeller.* Once during the season, remove the propeller and apply a new coat of gasket cement to the splined shaft. (See earlier detailed instructions.) If you operate in salt water, do this twice during the season or about every 60 days. Remember: when removing the propeller, follow the instructions for your particular motor in order to prevent accidental starting while you're at work. Replace the cotter pin if it

appears worn.

- *Drain and refill lower unit of motor* once a month. Check the condition of the oil which drains out each time. If it looks milky, water is leaking in and you may need a new gasket seal, which your mechanic should install; or correction may be as simple as installing a new washer on the holes.

- *Check and clean fuel filters.* There is no specified time for checking and cleaning the filters. If the motor begins to act up—is hard to start or runs fitfully—the filters are one of the first places to check. But it isn't a bad idea to put them on your maintenance schedule during the boating season.

- *Lubricate moving parts on outside of motor*—swivel pin, swivel bracket, clamp screws—every 60 days or once during the season. Take the cowl off and do the same for the linkages and parts under the hood which your manual says should be lubricated—also every 60 days.

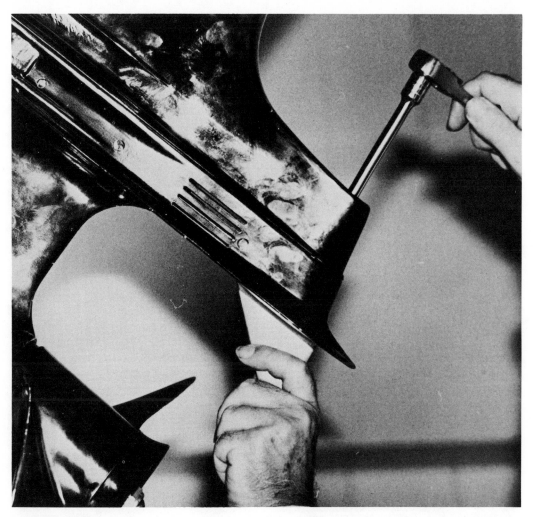

One boating problem is that when two different metals are close to each other in the water, a galvanic reaction takes place, creating a small electrical charge. This will eventually eat away one of the metals. Some motors have trim tabs made from a special zinc alloy that literally sacrifice themselves during such galvanic reactions, thus saving aluminum underwater parts. If your motor has such a trim tab, check it occasionally. You will see it gradually being eaten away. Replace it before it is reduced to half of its original size. The trim tab is inexpensive, and replacement is simple. A single bolt holds the tab in place. Use a long socket in a ratchet-type wrench to loosen the bolt as shown. Discard the old tab, put the new one in place, and use the wrench to tighten the bolt.

OPERATING YOUR BOAT EFFICIENTLY

The price of gasoline is climbing and from time to time the supply may be uncertain. In these days of energy consciousness, it behooves each of us to get the most performance out of each ounce of fuel we use. These, then, are three good reasons why you should find as many ways as possible to operate your craft at maximum efficiency.

Here are some good ways to get the most boating miles from the least amount of fuel:

- *Always keep your engine in tune.* When its timing gets out of adjustment, when the points are worn or burned, or when the spark plugs need to be regapped or have deposits on their electrodes,

you burn more gas at every speed.

- *Get the right propeller.* Every engine has a recommended operating range when running at full throttle. For instance, for the 1974 Johnson 70-horsepower motor, the operating range is 4,500 to 5,500 revolutions per minute. The correct propeller is one which puts the motor in the middle or upper half of this range, or for this motor, an RPM reading of 5,200 to 5,400. If the RPMs are too high or too low, the result is poor performance and poor economy.

With your dealer's help arrange several practice runs with different propellers. Use a stopwatch and make runs over the same distance to determine which

A full instrument panel not only makes for a good-looking boat but can also be a big help in getting the most miles per gallon of fuel. Install a tachometer and learn to use it in conjunction with your speedometer. You'll quickly find out which is the best speed for the most economical operation.

Overpowered and overloaded boats cause accidents and cause you to use much more fuel than you should. Look for the Boating Industry Association's plate in your boat. It tells you the maximum horsepower you should have for your particular boat type, the maximum weight of your passengers, and the total maximum weight your boat will carry. Observe these limits carefully and you may save your life and the lives of your passengers. Weight and horsepower limits may not seem important as you sit at the dock, but if you hit rough water, encounter a severe storm, or even operate at maximum speed, they could become vital to your safety.

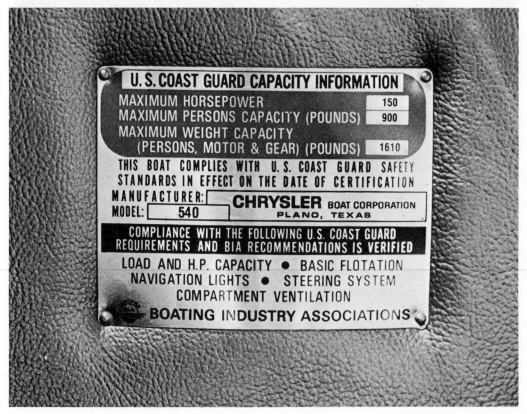

One way to save precious fuel is to use a small electric trolling motor when fishing. Trolling with your big outboard uses too much fuel. The little electric motor, run by a battery, will move the boat at a nice, slow, effective trolling speed. Here, in the picture, the boat has a bow-mounted trolling motor. It swings up onto the boat for normal cruising with the big outboard.

Far left:
Maintenance of electric trolling motors is relatively simple and consists chiefly of regular lubrications—every 60 days when operated in fresh water and every 30 days in salt water. No lubrication is applied to the inside of the motor but to transom clamps and other exterior working parts. No work need be done under the little motor's hood for winter storage either. The motor's manual will specify what exterior points need to be lubricated and the proper lubricant.

Left:
Another way to get the most out of your outboard is to keep the propeller in good shape. Check it regularly to see that no weeds have become wound around the shaft. Smooth out rough edges and small nicks with a medium grade of sandpaper. If the nicks are deep, or if they have changed the contour of the blades, it is best to get a new propeller.

propeller works best for your rig.

- *Keep your propeller in good shape.* When the edges become nicked, the efficiency of the prop is reduced and you get less miles per gallon. Check occasionally to see that weeds have not collected around the prop or the shaft.
- *Use a tachometer.* The tachometer is an instrument which gives a constant reading of your engine speed in revolutions per minute. Using it in conjunction with a speedometer, you can quickly determine which is the best speed for economizing fuel.
- *Adjust your engine to the correct height.* Engine height is important: the higher an outboard is mounted on the boat's transom, the less drag there will be from the lower unit. In most cases, the cavitation plate on the lower unit should be even with the bottom of the boat. But in some cases, depending on hull weight and configuration, it could be up to 2½ inches below the bottom of the boat. Check your dealer for advice on this.
- *Adjust the trim tab.* Larger outboard motors have a small trim tab on the lower unit. It can be adjusted to offset propeller torque and make steering easier. If it is presently adjusted so that it creates a drag, it will cut your fuel economy. The adjustment can be made quickly with a small wrench.
- *Adjust the tilt angle of your motor.* The tilt angle is the angle between the motor and the boat's transom. Some big motors have a power tilt mechanism. Others are adjusted manually, and there are usually five available positions. The adjustment on these motors is made by setting the tilt locking pin or stop lever.

In normal operating position, the tilt angle should be adjusted so that the lower unit is straight up and down when the boat is running at top speed. If the motor is tilted inward, too close to the transom, the bow of the boat will dig into the water and "plow." This makes turning difficult and flooding easier.

If the motor is tilted too far out from the transom, the boat "squats" in the water and will tend to "gallop," in which case steering may be skittish. You may even get a condition known as "cavitation" in which the propeller spins in a trough instead of in the water.

The best way to determine the right tilt angle for your boat is to make some practice runs at different tilt angle settings. If the boat plows (runs with the bow down), move the tilt adjustment away from the transom one notch and try again. If the boat "gallops" (runs with the bow high), move the tilt adjustment one notch toward the transom and try again. You'll get a more efficient use of your fuel dollar when the boat runs almost level but with the bow slightly up.

- *Balance your load.* One method of getting your boat to run at the correct level is to rearrange the weight distribution. Move the gear and passengers as necessary, concentrating the weight toward the rear of the boat so that less horsepower is required to keep the bow out of the water.
- *Clean the bottom of your boat.* Manufacturers have made some hull tests and come up with astonishing results in regard to the effect of a dirty boat bottom on both speed and fuel economy. Evinrude reports that road film and tar on a boat that has been trailered even a short distance can cut the top speed of the boat by 2 miles an hour.

They also say that a boat moored for 30 days in salt water

Trimming A Boat

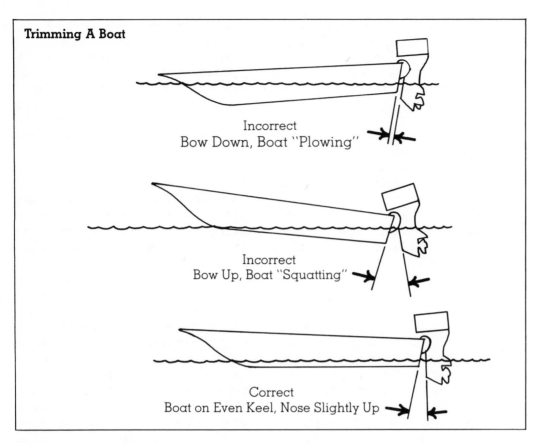

Incorrect
Bow Down, Boat "Plowing"

Incorrect
Bow Up, Boat "Squatting"

Correct
Boat on Even Keel, Nose Slightly Up

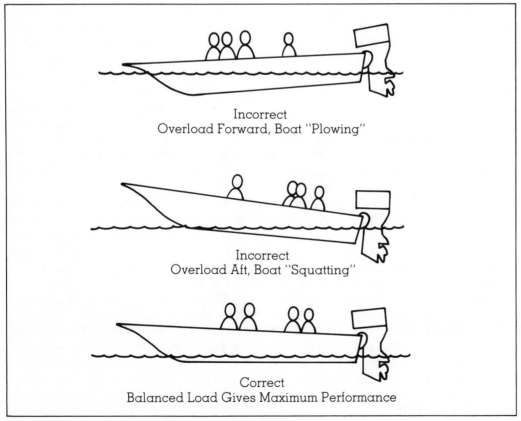

Incorrect
Overload Forward, Boat "Plowing"

Incorrect
Overload Aft, Boat "Squatting"

Correct
Balanced Load Gives Maximum Performance

had its top speed dropped from 26.5 miles per hour down to 18 miles per hour. The loss was less for the same boat, a 16-foot fiber glass job with a 35-horsepower motor, in fresh water—but was still significant.

To get top speed and more miles per gallon, keep the bottom of your boat clean. (For more on this subject, see Chapter V, "Hull Maintenance.")

- *Keep the throttle back.* Your boat runs best in every respect at less than full throttle. Every boat is a bit different, but generally speaking, the last 20 percent of throttle can cost you 30 to 40 percent in fuel.

Give the boat the throttle it needs to start planing; then start throttling back slowly. Do this until you are going as slowly as possible while keeping the boat on a solid, comfortable plane. If the boat starts to slip off its plane, increase the throttle slightly. You'll notice two things. One is that you don't suffer a big loss of speed. And the other is that your motor will sound as if it is hardly working. You'll save a remarkable amount of fuel this way.

There are a few other things you can do to save fuel and improve the efficiency of your boat: for example, don't change speeds excessively. Around the boatyard, the throttle jockey who rams his control constantly is known as a cowboy.

A boat runs most efficiently when on plane, so don't run off plane any more than you can help. Don't overload the boat with either gear or passengers. This is good safety advice as well as economy advice. Obviously, the more weight the motor has to push, the more fuel it will use.

If you do a lot of trolling, use a small trolling motor. Trolling with a big motor uses too much fuel. And finally, check your prop and lower unit regularly for weeds. Often, the prop will turn and drive your boat in spite of a collection of weeds wound around it. But when it does, it uses a lot more power and fuel to give you the speed you want.

TROUBLESHOOTING

If you do a good job of maintaining your boat, you will cut breakdowns to a minimum. But it is a sad fact of life that even tender loving care won't prevent mechanical illness from striking sooner or later. If it happens when you are a long way from home and a marina with a mechanic, then you must be the doctor who administers first aid.

Every mechanical problem can be divided into two parts—the diagnosis of the problem and the repair of the problem. Diagnosis may be the more important of the two, because after a correct analysis you should know whether you can make the repairs yourself on the spot, or whether you need professional help. If you know you need professional help, don't waste time puttering, but instead look for ways of getting ashore or getting a repair boat out to you.

The troubleshooting chart at the end of this chapter was designed to help you make a good diagnosis of trouble. Look down the list of symptoms until you identify one that is similar to what has happened to you. Then look at the list of possible causes and check them out on your boat. You may be able to correct the problem in minutes.

Dealers tell us that a percentage of service calls turn out to be simple, and in many cases, if the skipper had checked carefully before calling for help, the call wouldn't have been necessary. A good many turn out to be as simple as an empty gas tank, a pinched gas line, or a closed gas tank vent.

Don't be caught in this embarrassing situation. Check out the simple and obvious items before you yell for help.

TROUBLESHOOTING CHART FOR YOUR OUTBOARD MOTOR

If your motor has trouble, the problem may be something simple you can easily correct yourself—or you may need a professional. Before calling for help, locate the symptoms in this chart and check the suggested causes. Then, if you can't solve the problem, get help.

Symptom	Possible Cause
Electric starter does not work.	1. Loose wiring or corroded connections. 2. Battery terminals corroded. 3. Weak battery. (Problem could be that the alternator is not charging the battery.) 4. Broken wire or wire with frayed insulation in wiring harness.
Electric starter does not work, but clicks.	1. Loose wiring or corroded connections. 2. Weak battery. 3. Loose wire on starter motor. 4. Broken wire in electrical harness.
Motor is hard to start.	1. Empty gas tank. 2. Gas tank air vent not open. 3. Fuel lines kinked. (See if the gas tank is pinching the fuel line.) 4. Water or dirt in fuel system. Check fuel filters in tank and motor. 5. Failure to choke the motor. 6. Failure to prime the motor. 7. Damaged wires or loose or corroded connections. 8. Loose fuel connector. 9. Cracked distributor cap or rotor. 10. Motor needs a tune-up. 11. Spark plugs need to be cleaned and gapped.
Motor misses at low speed or won't idle smoothly.	1. Too much or not enough oil in fuel. 2. Motor needs to be timed. 3. Carburetor idle needs adjusting. 4. Needs new breaker points. 5. Loose or broken ignition wires. 6. Spark plugs need to be cleaned and gapped. 7. Cracked distributor cap or rotor. 8. Fuel pump diaphragm punctured. 9. Faulty ignition switch.
Motor misses at high speeds.	1. Spark plugs need to be cleaned and gapped. 2. Loose, leaking, or broken ignition wires. 3. Needs new breaker points. 4. Water in fuel. 5. Motor needs to be timed.
Motor coughs, spits, or slows.	1. Idle or high speed needle set too lean. 2. Carburetor not synchronized. 3. Fuel lines obstructed or leaking. 4. Fuel pump diaphragm punctured. 5. Worn or leaking fuel connector.

Symptom	Possible Cause
Motor vibrates excessively or runs rough and smokes.	1. Idle or high speed needle valves set too rich. 2. Too much oil in fuel. 3. Carburetor not synchronized. 4. Choke not opening properly. 5. Fuel float level too high. 6. Air passage to carburetor obstructed. 7. Transom bracket clamps loose on transom. 8. Prop out of balance. 9. Broken motor mount.
Motor slows and stops after running well for short period.	1. Weeds or other debris on propeller or lower unit. 2. Insufficient cooling water. Check water intake for blockage. 3. Water or oil in fuel system. Check fuel filters in tank and motor. 4. Lower unit needs lubricating. 5. Gas tank air vent not open. 6. Not enough oil in fuel. 7. Spark plugs fouled, causing pre-ignition. 8. Slow speed adjustment too rich or too lean.
Motor will not start, kicks back, backfires into lower unit.	1. Spark plug wires reversed. 2. Flywheel gear sheared. 3. Motor needs to be timed and synchronized.
Motor will not accelerate. Low top RPM.	1. Carburetor needs adjusting. 2. Motor needs to be timed. 3. Spark plugs need to be cleaned and gapped. 4. Needs new breaker points. 5. Loose or broken ignition wires. 6. Weeds on lower unit or propeller. 7. Not enough oil in lower unit. 8. Not enough oil in fuel. 9. Fuel line restricted in some manner.
Motor will not accelerate. Starts and idles well, but dies down when power applied.	1. High or low speed needle set too lean. 2. Dirt in needle valves. 3. Choke partly closed. 4. Motor needs to be timed and synchronized. 5. Fuel lines obstructed or kinked. 6. Not enough oil in fuel. 7. Breaker points dirty, worn, or burned. 8. Spark plugs need to be cleaned and gapped.
Motor will not deliver power under heavy load.	1. Weeds or other debris on propeller or lower unit. 2. Wrong prop for load. 3. Breaker points burned or dirty. 4. Prop hub slips.
Motor overheats.	1. Motor not deep enough in water. 2. Not enough oil in fuel. 3. Gas and oil improperly mixed. 4. Faulty thermostat.

Symptom	Possible Cause
Motor overheats (continued)	5. Insufficient cooling water. Plugged water intake on lower unit. 6. Bad water pump impeller, plate, housing, or seal. 7. Improper ignition timing. Have engine tuned.
Motor stops suddenly, freezes up.	1. Empty gas tank. 2. Not enough oil in fuel. 3. Insufficient cooling water. Bad water pump or motor run with water intakes blocked. 4. Lower unit needs lubricating. 5. Bent or broken rod, crankshaft, driveshaft, prop shaft, or stuck piston.
Motor knocks excessively.	1. Too much or not enough oil in fuel. 2. Flywheel nut loose. 3. Bent shift rod. 4. Loose assemblies, bolts, or screws.
Battery not being charged.	1. Battery dead; needs replacing. Check with hydrometer to ascertain condition. 2. Connections to generator or alternator loose or dirty. 3. Drive belt loose or broken. 4. Faulty voltage regulator or cutout relay. 5. Blown fuse. 6. Bad generator or alternator.
Motor uses too much fuel.	1. Fuel pump diaphragm punctured. 2. Carburetor gaskets need replacing. 3. Loose distributor pulley. 4. Fuel tank or fuel lines leaking.

This list does not attempt to show every possible problem which might arise. Rather, the list is designed to point out those troubles you might discover and correct yourself, before turning to a professional mechanic to handle the more complicated remedies. Many problems are caused by serious defects within the motor workings which you can't reach without taking the unit apart. In such cases, see an experienced mechanic.

Postseason Motor Maintenance

Like it or not, the boating season eventually comes to an end—at least in many parts of the country—and you have to put your rig away until next year. The maintenance work you do at this time can be a critical factor as to how well the motor will run next year.

An alternative to mothballing the rig yourself is to take the boat and motor to your marine dealer. Let him do the whole job, including both preparation and actual storage. For many people, this is the best way.

The other way is to do the job yourself. If you have a summer home with a boathouse, you can store the rig in it. Or you can trailer the whole thing home and store it in the garage, driveway, or backyard. If you do either of these, you must do the mothballing operation yourself.

The first problem is how to store the motor. It should be stored in the upright position, secured from possibly tipping over, and it should be covered—but with a cover which can "breathe." All water should be drained from it, since trapped water could freeze and expand, cracking the gear or water pump housing.

Any motor of 50 horsepower or over is big, heavy, and hard to handle. You can't exactly call such a motor "portable"—so why try to use it like a portable? Store the motor right on the boat. For safety's sake, and for the sake of your abdominal muscles, if you decide to lift one of the big motors, use a hoist or other lifting device.

You can store smaller motors on the boat, too. But they are small enough so that if you choose, you can lift them off the boat and store them indoors.

The original box in which the motor was delivered makes a good storage rack if you still have it. If not, you can build a case out of 2 x 4 lumber, or buy a ready-made unit. The important thing is to be sure the frame is strong and supports the motor off the floor by its clamp bracket.

MOTHBALLING THE MOTOR

While you are getting the boat ready for winter storage, you have an excellent opportunity to give it a thorough inspection. You may discover parts which should be replaced, paint work that ought to be done, and find other repair possibilities. You can do all of the work immediately or do some of it now and schedule the rest for the spring. The important thing is to note the areas requiring attention in your maintenance log as a reminder.

You'll find a section in your motor manual on how to prepare the motor for winter storage. *Follow the manufacturer's instructions.* The following step-by-step outline is general and not intended to replace the manufacturer's recommendations.

- *Protect the interior of the motor.* To do this, you must get rust preventive into the cylinders. Each motor manufacturer recommends a slightly different method for doing this, and the method is outlined in your motor operating manual. Follow these instructions. But regardless of the motor make, the objective is the same in each case: to distribute rust-preventive oil through the cylinders and leave it there throughout the storage period.

- *Drain all water from the water pump.* With the motor in its upright position, remove the cowl. Pull the throttle back all the way and disconnect the spark plug wires. Check to see that nothing is blocking the water intake ports in the lower unit. Now, manually rotate the motor's flywheel several times. This will exhaust the water from the pump.

   If you have operated your boat in salt water, and if your operating manual recommends it, flush

You can store your outboard motor right on the boat. Larger motors—those over 50 horsepower—are big, heavy, and hard to handle. Do not attempt to lift one without the help of a hoist or other lifting device. This boat will be stored here in the yard beside the house.

Before storing your rig for the winter, clean the motor's powerhead. If there is an accumulation of oily dirt, spray the powerhead with Gunk or another emulsifier, then rinse it with water according to the instructions on the label. Allow the motor to dry thoroughly, and then give it a final spray of rust preventive. You can buy rust preventive in convenient spray cans. *Note:* When rinsing the emulsifier from the power head, cover the carburetor. Do not allow water to enter the carburetor.

Right:
One essential part of getting your motor ready for winter storage is to drain and refill the lower unit. The old lubricant may have water in it which can cause corrosion during the storage period. After the draining has been completed, clean the unit.

Far right:
The final job when getting your motor ready for storage is to give the entire motor a light coating of oil or wax. If you find nicks or scratches which need to be retouched, do this with touch-up paint before applying the protective coating of wax.

In recent years outboard motor manufacturers have begun to use metals which resist the corrosive action of salt water in the construction of the lower units, but some motors require a freshwater flushing after saltwater operation. It is a good idea to at least rinse off all outboard equipment, including the boat and the trailer, after contact with salt water. If your motor requires a freshwater flushing, you can purchase a special fitting—shown here—which permits you to use an ordinary garden hose to wash out the lower unit.

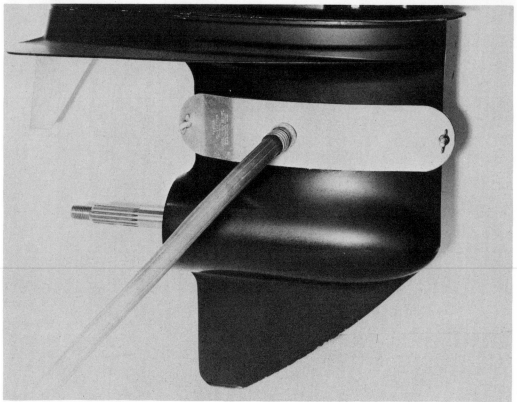

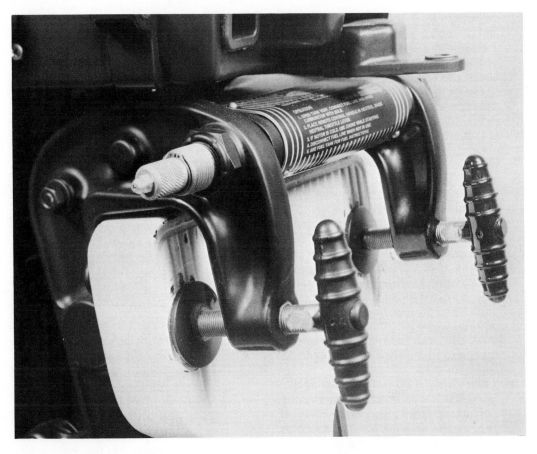

Check your motor over for small grease fittings such as the one shown here: the small white fitting on the end of the tilt mechanism. Each of these fittings must be lubricated with a small grease gun, which fits on the end of a tube of lubricant and which is available from your marine dealer. Be familiar with the location of each such fitting, and when doing motor maintenance, be sure not to overlook applying lubricant to each one.

the cooling system with fresh water before storage. You'll need a flush testing device—a clamp which fits around the lower unit and directs the fresh water into the ports—which attaches to a garden hose. Some motors no longer require flushing, but others do.

- *Drain the carburetor float chamber.* Get rid of all gasoline in the motor by draining the float chamber. Remove the fuel filter bowl, drain it, and inspect the filter element; clean it if necessary; then reinstall it.
- *Store fuel only after adding a stabilizing compound.* Should you, or shouldn't you store fuel over the winter? You should *not* store it without precautionary treatment—the addition of a stabilizing compound—or it will get gummy and cause no end of trouble next spring. Also, you should not store a partially-filled tank of fuel; the empty portion will

rust over an extended storage period. Either empty the tank completely, or add stabilizer and fill it all the way.

Experienced boatmen who have had trouble with stored fuel in the past prefer not to store it but plan instead to begin each boating season with a full tank of new fuel. If there is fuel left over in the boat's tank at the end of the season, they burn it in their cars. The oil in the outboard fuel won't disturb the way a car runs if the fuel is added to the car's tank a gallon or so at a time.

One thing is sure: with energy sources at a premium, no one should waste any gasoline. If you store outboard motor fuel without adding a stabilizer, you will waste it.

- *Clean and spray the powerhead inside the cowl.* If the powerhead has an accumulation of oily dirt on it, spray it with Gunk or another emulsifier, rinse, then dry thoroughly. If the motor is fairly clean, simply wipe off all dirt; then spray it with a coating of rust preventive.

- *Drain the lower unit of motor.* Use the normal procedure as described in Chapters 2 and 3 to drain and refill the lower unit. It is particularly important to put new lubrication in at this time because this will eliminate any water, salt or fresh, which might have gotten into the lower unit. If water is left in over the winter, it could cause corrosion, and it could freeze, expand, and crack vital motor parts.
- *Check the propeller.* This is a good time to look the prop over for damage and to have it repaired or replaced. Even if it seems to be in good shape, pull it off and put new gasket cement on the splined shaft; then replace the propeller.
- *Coat motor with a light film of oil.* Look the motor over for nicks and scratches. If you find any, retouch them now or wait until spring as you choose. Then wipe the entire motor with a clean cloth soaked in light oil. This puts a protective coating of oil over the motor. Some manufacturers recommend a coat of automobile wax instead of oil; either will do the job.
- *Disconnect spark plug cables.* By leaving the cables disconnected you'll avert the possibility of accidentally starting the motor. Some manufacturers recommend that spark plugs be removed and cleaned or replaced before storage. You can either do this task now or wait until preseason maintenance in the spring.
- *Store motor in an upright position under a ventilated cover* to prevent moisture from condensing under the cover and causing corrosion.

MOTHBALLING THE BATTERY

Taking good care of your boat's battery will prolong its usefulness. Never store the battery in the boat; bring it into your garage. Be sure the storage area isn't airtight but has normal ventilation.

Incidentally, if you've ever watched mechanics around a service station handle a battery, you've seen that they pick it up and carry it with a device that looks like a strap with a hole in either end. These strap carriers are inexpensive and make it a lot easier to carry the battery without spillage or damage. You can buy one in any automotive supply store.

- *Clean the battery case.* Use a solvent or cleaner (your dealer has one) to remove all grease and dirt from the battery case. Use the battery post cleaning tool to remove any sulfate (white residue) from the battery posts and battery terminal clamps.
- *Check the condition of the battery.* There isn't much point in storing a battery all winter if you have to replace it in the spring. Use a hydrometer to check the condition of the battery. When the specific gravity reading on the hydrometer goes below 1.230, the battery should be recharged. A charge should bring the reading up to 1.260. If, after charging the battery, the reading doesn't change, you need a new battery. If it comes only part way up, be wary. The battery is in its terminal stages, and buying a new one is recommended.
- *Cover battery plates with distilled water* if water is low. Regular water leaves a mineral residue as it evaporates which prevents your battery from functioning properly. Never overfill a battery. You should be able to see the water just above the plates. CAUTION: Battery acid is caustic and can burn your skin and injure your eyes. Work carefully and don't spill or splash the electrolyte.
- *Cover the battery terminals* with a heavy grease or petroleum jelly. This protects them against corro-

sion and prevents the discharge of electricity over the surface of the battery.

- *Store the battery.* Put the battery in a dry carton and store it in a cool, dry place.
- *Check water level* and recharge battery every 60 days. Any lead storage battery slowly loses its charge when stored. During the winter, check the water level of the battery about once every 60 days, and put the unit on a trickle charger at 6 amperes for 5 to 6 hours. Do not fast charge. Note that as the battery discharges, it becomes subject to freezing. If you allow it to discharge completely and it freezes, the water will expand and destroy the lead plates and the case.

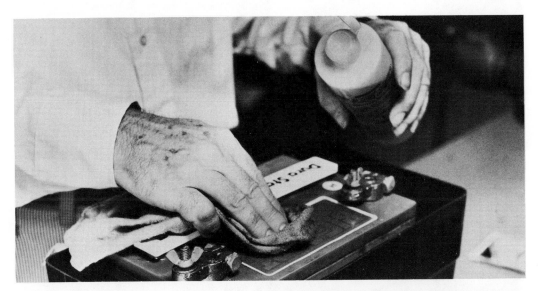

When getting the battery ready for winter storage, begin by cleaning the case thoroughly. Simply wipe it down with a cloth, or use a special cleaning solution designed to help get rid of any oily buildup.

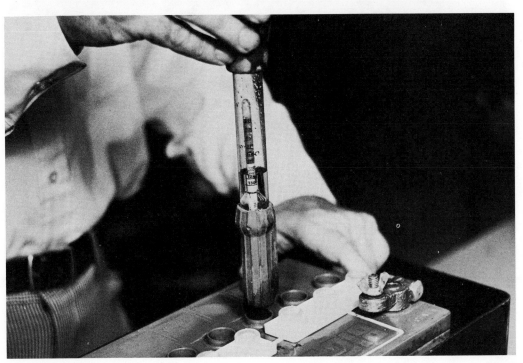

Find out how the battery survived the boating season by checking it with a hydrometer. It should be fully charged, with the hydrometer reading 1.260 specific gravity, when you store the battery for the winter. If it is low, have it charged before storage. If after charging the reading does not come up to 1.260, you'll probably need a new battery for the next boating season.

Just before putting the battery on the shelf for the winter, coat the terminal posts with a thick grease or petroleum jelly as a protective measure against corrosion.

Carry the battery carefully when removing it from the boat. The electrolyte is an acid and should not be spilled. This battery came with its own built-in carrying handles. However, if yours has no handles, you can buy a very inexpensive plastic strap which fits over the battery posts and serves as a handle. All automotive stores carry them, and they are safer than trying to pick the battery up in your hands.

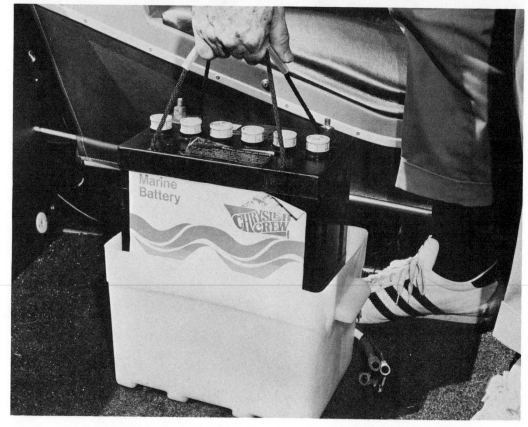

Hull
Maintenance

A leathery and grizzled old seaman—an iron man left over from the days of the wooden square riggers—once explained why sailors always thought of a ship as "she."

"It was because," he growled with a male chauvinist glint, "her rigging was worth more than her hull."

Times have changed in more ways than one. Now the hull is definitely worth more than the rigging, and if he had made that statement today, the old tar would be picketed. Even though there is a lot less rigging today, most sailors still think of their boats as feminine and give them the tender loving care due a lady.

Basically, taking care of your boat's hull means work in three categories: cleaning, painting, and repairing. There will be a good many seasons when getting your boat ready for water takes no more than a thorough cleaning and a few minor repairs. That's the routine we will deal with now. Later, we'll get into painting and major repairs.

CLEANING

Your boat has probably been sitting gathering dirt for half a year. Before that she probably spent nearly half a year in the water. And unless you gave her a pretty thorough scrubdown before putting the wraps on last fall, she's due for a bath.

The bath comes before you decide whether or not to paint her, and before you begin any repairs. It makes no difference whether your boat is fiber glass, aluminum, or wood. Use a mild detergent in warm water, some cloths, and a brush with moderately soft bristles to do the work.

You'll find a number of cleaning compounds at your marine dealer, from soaps and detergents through strong stuff designed to get at tough stains and spots. But household cleaning products will do the job, too. Detergents used around the kitchen sink and the typical pumice-type cleansers are fine.

Start at the top of the boat and work down, swabbing the cleaning stuff on and letting it stand for a while. Then go over each area with the brush and cloths to loosen the dirt. Finally, rinse thoroughly with a hose. One of the key secrets when using any cleaning compound for any purpose is: give it a little time to work. The "one quick wipe" routine does not give the chemicals a chance to do what they were designed to do.

Wash the inside and the outside of the boat. If you have a canvas top, rinse the accumulated dirt off. You may have received special cleaning instructions with it. If so, read them and follow the directions.

After the final rinse, examine the boat for special cleaning problems: stains which resisted the normal washing. Some of them will give in to a gentle rubbing with a sink cleanser. Others may need a stain remover or a mild solvent. Oil, grease, and algae stains at or below the water line may call for a household detergent with a mild bleaching action.

Be careful when using any cleaning compound. Don't use harsh or heavy-duty chemicals or detergents. Apply any abrasive gently, even the sink cleanser.

After the bath, and if no repairs need to be made, follow the maintenance procedure that applies to your boat's hull type.

• *Fiber glass hulls.* Apply a good automotive wax. If you use a

To start the new boating season, give your rig a good bath. Washing is not just a matter of getting her to look shipshape; a clean hull runs better and uses less fuel. Use a mild detergent in warm water, and then rinse with the garden hose.

If you find spots which will not come clean with a simple washing with detergent, use a brush with moderately soft bristles to scrub them. Marine dealers sell cleaning compound for such areas, too, but be careful of abrasive cleaners on fiber glass hulls. The gel coat, or top layer, of the fiber glass is fairly soft and scratches easily. With pumice-type kitchen sink cleaners, use a soft cloth and rub gently to get the spot out. Do not rub as if you were cleaning the kitchen sink.

When the hull is clean, apply a coat of automobile wax. Paste wax probably does the best job although the liquid waxes, which are easier to apply and don't require as much rubbing and buffing, will certainly work.

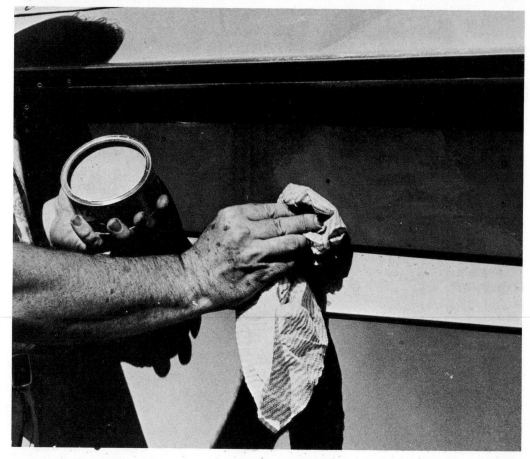

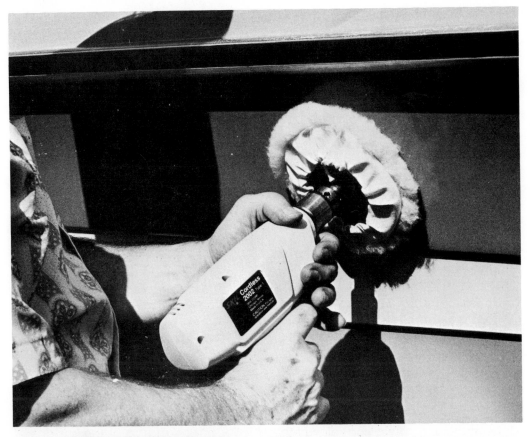

An easy way to buff and polish the new wax is with a buffing pad attachment on an electric drill. This particular drill is one of the new cordless types, a particularly handy tool for boaters because you can use it around water without fear of electrical shock. You should never stand in water beside your boat holding a regular, cord-type electric drill because you may electrocute yourself. You can, however, stand in water while holding a cordless drill.

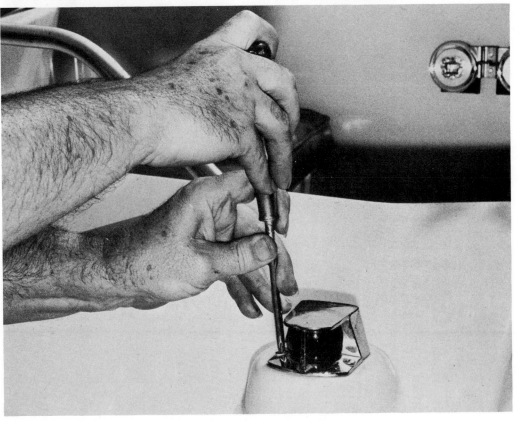

When getting the boat ready for mothballs, check all the fittings. This is a good time to find those which have become loose during the season. While you are at it, switch all lights on and check for burned-out bulbs. Replace any broken or bent cleats and tierings. Any work you do now will save time and effort next spring.

power tool to buff the wax, be very careful not to overheat the surface. Use a touch-and-go technique, and keep the buffer moving.

- *Aluminum hulls*. Natural aluminum hulls have been treated with a clear protective coating and then given a wax coat at the factory to reduce normal oxidation. You may wish to apply an automobile wax for extra protection. Painted aluminum hulls need to be washed carefully with a mild soap or detergent. Be particularly wary of gritty cleansers and solvents because you can cut through the paint to the metal quite easily. When the hull is clean, give it a coat of wax.
- *Wooden hulls*. If the paint on the hull is sound, you are nearly ready to go. Check the sides and bottom for mars and bruises which might permit water to penetrate the wood, and touch these up to seal them. Apply a coat of wax to the decks—and you're finished.

When looking for minor repair jobs to do, check all the fittings, running lights, etc., for loose screws which should be tightened. Replace broken or bent cleats and tie-rings.

PAINTING

If you haven't already discovered it, you should be aware of the fact that painting a boat is a very complex business. You have a wide choice of products to select from. Some paints require primers and some don't. Different paints are often used on wood, aluminum, and fiber glass. And if you run your boat in salt water or leave it in fresh water for long periods of time, you must think about antifouling bottom paints.

To help clarify things, here are some basic rules about painting:

- *Compatibility*. Don't use a primer by one maker and a finish coat by another. Use only the primer or undercoat recommended on

the label of the final coat paint. Otherwise, the final coat may adhere poorly to the primer coat causing it to blister and peel.

Read the labels and literature and ask the salesman about what material each paint may be applied to. Some paints are for wood, but not for fiber glass; some should not be used on aluminum. Some paints which work on wood also work on fiber glass if a specific type of primer is used first. Most marine paint manufacturers clearly state which surfaces their paints are for—and which they are not for.

- *Surface preparation*. Much of the success of any paint job depends on how well you prepare the surface. You must get all the grease and wax off, for example, or the new paint won't adhere. The surface must be free of dirt, dust, and moisture, or you may get interesting bumps, bubbles, or blisters. A light sanding of the surface, if called for, provides "tooth" for the new paint—a slightly rough surface which it can grip. Glossy painted surfaces—high-gloss enamels—must have the gloss removed by sanding or with a gloss-removing chemical, or the new paint will flake away.
- *Application tools*. Some coatings are best applied with a brush (varnish, for example) and some can be applied with a roller. Check the recommendations on the can or in the literature.
- *Application*. Follow the paint manufacturer's directions exactly. If two thin coats rather than one thicker coat are called for, apply the paint that way. Instructions on a paint can and in paint literature were written the hard way—based on experience. Each paint has different coating and drying characteristics, too. If you have been successful with one paint, don't assume you can use all

paints the same way. Paint manufacturers lose business when their paints fail, and that's why the instructions are written the way they are—to eliminate failures. When the label calls for two coats, it does *not* mean the manufacturer is trying to get you to use more paint. It means that two coats will do the best job.

- *Drying.* Drying times vary widely and the time mentioned on the label may or may not be valid. If you paint in very humid weather or if the weather is cool, drying time may be much longer than specified on the label. Give the paint plenty of time to dry. Remember that most paint also needs a curing time, usually lasting several weeks. During the curing period, the paint shouldn't be washed with detergents, scrubbed, or have anything applied to its surface.

There are four basic types of paints that are most widely used today, not including the antifouling bottom paints which will be discussed later.

- *Alkyd base.* This synthetic plastic paint is easy to apply and good for all-around marine use. It is relatively inexpensive, but softer and not as durable as other paint types. Do not use alkyd base paint on fiber glass.
- *Epoxy base.* Makes a chemical bond, and is good for use on fiber glass, wood, and metal hulls. Its tough coating resists oil and abrasion, but an epoxy base paint is expensive. The materials are mixed from a two-part package, and the paint must be applied when temperature is over 70° F. Apply epoxy base paint with a natural bristle brush; it will attack nylon bristles.
- *Vinyl base.* Adheres well, is resistant to weather and chemicals, and stands up well under traffic when used as a deck paint. Vinyl base paint is good on wood and

aluminum, but is not as good as epoxy on fiber glass.
- *Urethane base.* Urethane varnishes are extremely durable. Urethane base paints have great resistance to acids, water, alkalis, and solvents. Harder than alkyd-based paints, urethane base paints bond well on fiber glass and are easy to apply.

Which type of paint should you use? Talk with other skippers in your area to learn their experience with different paints; talk to your marine dealer, too. Epoxies are very popular as are the urethanes, especially urethane varnishes for the boat's brightwork. But every one of these paints has some advantage, from cost to durability, and so it becomes a matter of choice and of weighing advantages and disadvantages.

When buying, stay with reputable brand names, especially those which specialize in marine products.

ANTIFOULING PAINTS

If you leave your boat in the water for any length of time, its bottom soon collects barnacles, mussels, eel grass, and a variety of mosses. These are saltwater animals, but in fresh water the same thing happens with different things collecting at a somewhat slower rate.

All of these organisms make the bottom of your boat look terrible, but more importantly, they cut down tremendously on the boat's performance: they reduce its top speed and increase gasoline consumption.

To combat bottom fouling, boaters use an antifouling paint on the boat bottom from the waterline down. Antifouling paints are actually poisonous paints—poisonous to the marine organisms which like to attach themselves to boat bottoms.

If you normally keep your boat on a trailer except when actually under way, you probably don't have to concern yourself with antifouling paint. If your boat stays in salt water, and especially warm salt water, you certainly must apply the protective paint. If your boat stays in fresh water, you should give the idea of using an antifouling paint very serious consideration.

There is a wide range of antifouling paints available. The old standby has been a copper-bearing paint, and there are formulations for different boating areas because some paints work better in warm water and against certain organisms. The old copper paints cannot be applied to aluminum because they are a different metal and set up a galvanic reaction. Nor can copper paints be applied to fiber glass—they will not stick to it.

There are antifouling paints now made, however, for use on aluminum and fiber glass boats. Just be sure to do some thorough researching—find out which paints are for each type of surface and which paints have proved effective in your area. An antifouling paint which works in New England may not do the job in Florida. And according to the experts at Pettit Paint Company, what worked three years ago in an area may not work this year. They make regional formulations and worry about changing the formulae to keep them effective.

Following instructions on the label is doubly important with specialized paints such as this. Do *exactly* as instructed, with absolutely no variation. However, the application isn't difficult, certainly no more difficult than that of any other paint.

PAINTING A FIBER GLASS BOAT

One of the great things about fiber glass boats is that they are very easy to maintain. They should be waxed and buffed at the beginning of each season and preferably two or more times during the boating season. The longer the boating season and the more the boat is in the water, the more frequently it should be waxed.

To understand the care of fiber glass, you should understand the way the hull is made. A cross-section of the wall of the hull would show that glass fibers in plastic are the core, with an outer layer of plastic without glass fibers. This outer layer is called the "gel coat." The gel coat is heavily pigmented and gives the boat its rich color. Waxing protects the surface and color of the gel coat.

The gel coat is fairly soft and scratches easily. Fine scratches dull the color and give the hull a worn appearance. Sometimes, a treatment with fiber glass boat polish will improve its appearance. If this doesn't help, try fiber glass rubbing compound, a very mild abrasive which cuts off the outer layer of the dulled gel coat.

In time, fiber glass colors fade. This usually takes several seasons in the sun, but it happens because the material is translucent, allowing the sun to get at the pigments. There comes a time when the total effect of scratching, gel coat removal, and fading makes a fiber glass boat look old and disreputable.

This is when the hull should be painted to restore its new, sharp look. As you read earlier, there are vinyl, urethane, and epoxy paints which adhere to fiber glass. The epoxies are the most popular because of their exceptional adhesion and hard finish. No primers are necessary with epoxies. Proper preparation of the surface, however, is essential.

Follow the paint manufacturer's instructions carefully. In general, this is the technique:

1. Sand the surface thoroughly; then wash with a strong scouring cleanser and rinse with clear water.
2. When dry, sand once more with a fine garnet paper. This gives the surface the "tooth" for good adhesion.
3. Apply the paint according to manufacturer's directions. Epoxy paint shouldn't be used when the temperature is below 70°.

Fiber glass hulls are easy to care for; often, for many years, they need no more maintenance than a good washing and waxing. But in time the outer gel coat will become seriously scratched and dull. Over a period of time the sun will fade the original color, adding to a developing sad appearance. Then it is time to paint the hull to restore its good looks. The first job is to sand the hull thoroughly. Remember that fiber glass sands readily so that a few passes with a power sander are usually all that is needed. Be sure to sand the entire surface. Incidentally, do not breathe the dust. Work in a well-ventilated area and wear a mask.

After sanding, wash the surface with a scouring cleanser and rinse thoroughly. The object is to remove all of the glass dust. Allow the surface to dry, and go over the surface with a fine garnet sandpaper to provide tooth for the coat of paint. Wipe the surface clean and then apply the paint according to the directions on the can. Most boaters today prefer epoxy paints for fiber glass hulls; these must be applied when the temperature is above 70°F. Be sure to follow directions carefully.

Temperature affects drying time: the cooler the day, the longer the drying time required.

Now there are epoxy paints with antifouling properties available, so if your boat needs bottom protection, you might consider one of these.

PAINTING OTHER SURFACES

- *Vinyl deck surfaces and vinyl cabin tops.* Wash the surface and then rinse thoroughly. Do not sand. Apply a coat of vinyl and canvas primer; after it dries (usually about 4 hours), sand very lightly and apply finish coat, which can be a marine epoxy enamel. Two coats are best, with 24 hours of drying time between coats.
- *Wood decks.* For a top job, sand down to bare wood, then apply a sealer. After it is dry, sand lightly and apply an undercoat. The type of undercoat and drying

time should be determined by the final coat paint you select. One of the epoxy paints made for decks would work well.

If you want to maintain the high gloss, natural wood effect of wood decks or other trim, investigate the urethane or epoxy varnishes. Usually the directions will tell you to sand to bare wood and then apply a stain-filler, followed several hours later by a clear sealer. Apply two final coats of the varnish, allowing ample drying time between coats.

Once again—remember that you should use compatible products by the same manufacturer, and follow the accompanying directions exactly. Do not, for example, substitute a different primer product for the one specified on the label of the final coat product.

- *Metal.* Most of the time, the chrome and other metal attachments on a boat need only occasional

Chrome and metal fittings on your boat are easy to keep new looking with an occasional cleaning with a metal polish, followed by a protective wax coating. Wax is especially necessary if you operate your rig in salt water. You also can apply a spray coat of a thin, clear, metal-coating lacquer.

When everything else has been done, button the canvas and plastic up to keep the weather out. If your boat is the open type, without a self-cover such as this model, you can buy a cover to fit over it, and you can also buy a cover for your motor. Note that these covers should not be airtight but should be able to breathe so that excessive moisture does not accumulate under them.

polishing and a coat of wax to protect them. However, you'll find clear metal coating materials available to protect them from rust, oxidization, and the effects of salt water. A thin layer of coating material is all that is necessary, and this is usually best sprayed on. If you do the work with the item still mounted to the boat, be sure to cover everything around the object before spraying. It is best, however, to remove the part, spray it, and reinstall it after it has dried thoroughly.

MIDSEASON HULL MAINTENANCE

For the most part, maintenance during the boating season for any type of hull should consist of keeping it clean. This is especially true of the area below the water line. For wood hulls, watch for dents and scratches from dock bumping and other damaging practices. Use touch-up paint to seal such weak spots so water can't soak into the wood.

Aluminum boats need only to be cleaned periodically—especially after a run in salt water. Fiber glass hulls should be kept clean and be waxed a couple of times during the season.

Using the waxes available today, this doesn't take very long.

POSTSEASON HULL MAINTENANCE

Clean any hull, no matter what material, when you take the boat out of the water just before you store it for the winter. At this time, any dirt and marine organisms on the hull can still be removed without too much trouble. But if you neglect the clean-up job until spring, the mess will have hardened and will be a real headache.

After cleaning, wax aluminum and fiber glass hulls to protect them. Then button up the topsides and put a cover over the whole rig. The cover should protect the boat and motor—but it should be ventilated and not be airtight. Most ready-made boat covers have ventilation slits which permit air to enter but keep out the rain and snow.

If painting is necessary on a wood hull, fall is the best time for the job. The paint serves as a protective coating during the winter and doing the job now saves the work in the spring when you may be eager to get out on the water. If painting isn't necessary, simply clean the hull and put the cover on.

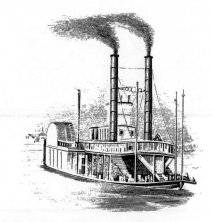

Hull Repairs

There is a lot of flotsam drifting in the waters in which you run your boat, some of it just beneath the surface and hard to see even when you are keeping a weather eye open. Hitting a submerged log or other large debris can damage your hull, even to the extent of putting a hole in it.

One of the kids could ram a dock, or another boater could zig when he should have zagged coming out of a marina. Whatever the cause, hull damage, like dented fenders on your car, can be a boating fact of life.

Repairing a hull isn't easy work, especially when you want the finished job to look as good as it did before the damage. Usually, you'll get the best results by having the work done professionally. This is no reflection on your abilities as a do-it-yourselfer. It's just that experience is a large factor in doing a good, smooth repair job.

WOOD HULL REPAIRS

There are several kinds of repairs which might be needed on wood hulls, ranging from stopping small leaks all the way up to rebuilding a smashed bow.

You may be able to handle the leaks yourself. First, check all screws and bolts in the area of the leak. By tightening these, sometimes the leak can be cured. You can also try sealants which are available at your marine dealer's. You may find the leak is due to problems in the caulking, in which case you may have to recaulk, at least in the area of the leak.

Plastic caulking compounds now available have good adhesion and stay flexible after application. They aren't difficult to use as long as you follow the directions. To make a caulk repair, use an awl to dig out the old caulk, then stuff the seam with candle-wicking—if the caulking compound you use requires it. Finally, apply the new caulk and repaint the area.

Hooks and rockers are tough problems. These are terms used to describe a wood hull which has warped or twisted slightly. This twist seriously affects the running ability of the boat, and so must be corrected, but it is a job for someone with experience. The basic idea is to get the hull wet, apply pressure to the affected area, and hold that pressure until the hull dries. The process is easier to describe than to do. Better turn the job over to a professional.

ALUMINUM HULL REPAIRS

You can take dents out of an aluminum hull by tapping carefully with a rubber mallet or by using automotive body tools. Tap gently, and start at the outer edges of the dent, working your way around its perimeter and then toward the center. In the case of severe dents, the metal may have been stretched, and the only way to make it shrink is with heat. The heat must be kept constant at around 500°, and the metal must be kept hot while it is worked back to its original contour. Keeping the right temperature and working the hot metal requires experience; do not try such a repair on an aluminum hull unless you know what you're doing.

Punctures in the hull can be fixed temporarily by first hammering the punctured area back to its proper contour and sealing the holes with fiber glass and resin. Repair kits with everything needed to do the job can be purchased from all marine dealers.

Temporarily repairing larger holes and permanently repairing smaller holes is made by applying an aluminum patch. First hammer the edges of the holes to restore the original contour. Then cut a patch of the same gauge (thickness) as the aluminum of the hull so that it overlaps the hole by about 1 inch on all sides.

Place the patch against the hole and shape it. Drill holes at the four corners, and use temporary fasteners to hold the patch in place. After the four fasteners are in place, remove them and apply a coat of caulk over the entire patch. Then refasten the patch to the hull with the temporary fasteners.

Rivet the patch to the hull with aluminum rivets as you remove the temporary fasteners. Drill a hole and insert a rivet; then hammer the rivet flat while holding a heavy piece of metal against the other side. Work progressively around the patch, installing one rivet after the other. When the riveting is finished, so is the job.

FIBER GLASS HULL REPAIRS

The most common repairs to fiber glass hulls are fixing gouges or deep scratches, cracks or crazes, and holes. Most marine dealers sell the necessary materials to do these jobs. The tools you need are a power disc sander, a power reciprocating sander, a sabre saw or keyhole saw, and a paint sprayer.

The repair work should be done at a temperature of 70° or higher, but should not be done in direct sunlight. The area should be well ventilated if indoors, because the polyester resins give off strong fumes.

After the fiber glass patch has been applied according to the directions accompanying the patch kit, use the sanding equipment to buff it smooth. This throws a dust composed of resin and glass into the air, where you can't help breathing it. Therefore, you should use a good respirator mask during grinding and finishing operations. Some people find their skin is sensitive to this dust, so it is also a good idea to wear clothes which cover your whole body. Gloves are good protection when handling resin.

- *Gouges and deep scratches.* Clean the area thoroughly with a detergent to get the wax off; then rinse with clear water and dry completely. The scratch or gouge can then be filled with an epoxy or polyester putty. If the gouge is more than ⅛ inch deep, mix some chopped glass fibers into the putty to reduce shrinkage and provide strength. Deep gouges are best handled by filling in two applications, the second after the first has set.

  After the final filler has been put into the gouge level with the hull surface, apply a sheet of plastic wrap to the surface with a squeegee or a roller. This will peel away after the resin has set and will give a smooth final finish.
- *Crazes and cracks.* Hairline cracks and spider-web crazes—the kind that often result from a hard blow against a fiber glass surface—are repaired with matching color paste. You buy this material to match the color of the boat—or at least as close to the color as you can get. Because sunlight causes the color in fiber glass to fade in time, there is little point in buying a color paste of the exact original color after the boat is a year or two old.

  For crazes, work the paste into the surface to fill the cracks. After it has set, wet sand the area with 600 grit sandpaper and then polish.

  For cracks, use a sharp knife to cut a V-shaped notch the length of the crack, and then fill the crack with the paste. If you think the crack might continue to spread, drill a small hole at each end. This will prevent further cracking. Fill the hole as well as the notch with paste; then allow the material to set, sand, and polish.
- *Holes.* You can buy kits which contain enough materials to patch small holes in fiber glass

hulls. The materials in these kits include the resin, a hardener which is mixed with the resin, fiber glass cloth, and fiber glass mat. The general idea is to build up a laminated patch using alternate pieces of cloth and mat soaked in the resin.

Begin the patch by cutting away all ragged material. Then "scarf," or bevel, the edges of the hole using a file or a power disc sander. Bevel from the inside of the hole only, so that the outside edge of the hole is smaller than the inside edge.

Now tape a back-up plate to the outside of the hole. Use cardboard or a piece of aluminum for this. The reason for the back-up plate is to give the patch you are going to make a surface against which to rest so that it will not sag.

You now have a cavity with beveled edges and a back. To make the patch, fill this cavity with successive layers of fiber glass cloth and mat. The outermost ply should be cloth—outermost meaning the exterior of the hull. Because the hole is scarfed, the first piece will be the smallest, and succeeding pieces will each be slightly larger. Cut these pieces of cloth and mat first, making sure they fit.

In the case of small patches, say up to 3 inches in diameter, the resin can be applied directly to the fiber glass after it has been placed in the break. If the patch is larger, it is a better idea to place the fiber glass (mat or cloth) on a sheet of plastic wrap, inpregnate it with resin, and then with the aid of the plastic, transfer it into the hole.

Use a stiff-bristled brush to work as much air as possible out of the resin as each layer is applied. A rubber or plastic squeegee does the job nicely on fiber glass cloth. Keep working steadily because

you want the entire patch completed within the gelling time of the resin.

If the patch is made in a hull which is more than 3/16 inch thick, it is better to do the job in two steps. Fill the patch area halfway, then let the patch material set before applying the rest of the fill. When the patch has been completed, let it cure according to the instructions on the resin can.

When the patch is hard, use the sander to smooth it out and blend it with the adjoining area. If you sand carefully, it should be difficult to see the patch or even feel it when you run your hand over the area.

The final problem is matching the color of the boat. This is done by applying a thin coat of color paste over the patched area. If the boat is quite new, you may be able to get a paste of the exact color from the manufacturer. If the boat is beginning to fade, you'll have to match the color by eye.

The best way to finish the repair is to paint the entire hull and thus avoid any color matching problems.

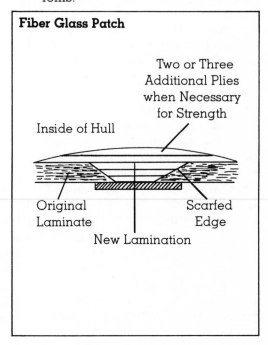

Fiber Glass Patch

Two or Three Additional Plies when Necessary for Strength

Inside of Hull

Original Laminate

Scarfed Edge

New Lamination

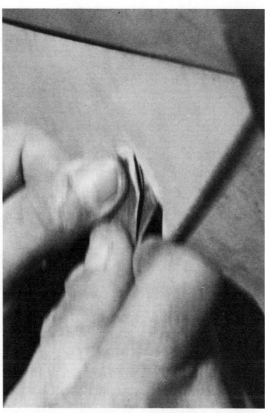

One of the most common repairs made on fiber glass hulls is patching deep gouges or scratches in the gel coat surface. This boat has a deep gouge near its bow. The first step is to clean out the damaged area and feather it into the surrounding part of the hull. Here a router bit in an electric drill is used to do the job. It could also have been done with a disc sander. Note that the damage is only in the gel coat; therefore neither the router nor sandpaper is allowed to dig into the under surface. All work is done in the gel coat only.

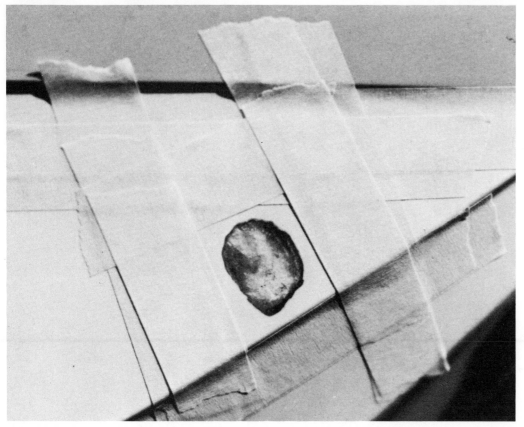

The next step is to clean away all dust and gel coat particles. Experts say to do a thorough job you should blow the area clean with compressed air, then wipe it with a cloth dipped in acetone. Next, use several layers of masking tape to build a little dam around the damaged area. Apply the repair material to the level of the masking tape so that the repaired area will be a little higher than the hull surface to allow for sanding down to a smooth and level finish.

Material used in repairing the gel coat is mixed with a catalyst; both the patch material and the catalyst are available at your marine dealer's. If you are working on a vertical surface—the side of the hull—you'll have to add a thickener to the gel coat so that it won't run out of the damaged area. A mixture of half thickener and half gel coat should be about right. Mix the thickener with the gel coat before adding the catalyst. Your dealer can provide the thickener. Follow mixing directions on the can, and remember that this work must be done at 70°F. or higher so that the gel coat will cure. Use a flat wooden tongue depressor to apply the gel coat-catalyst combination to the repair. Finally, cover the repaired area with a piece of plastic wrap as shown here. The gel coat won't cure if it is in contact with the air.

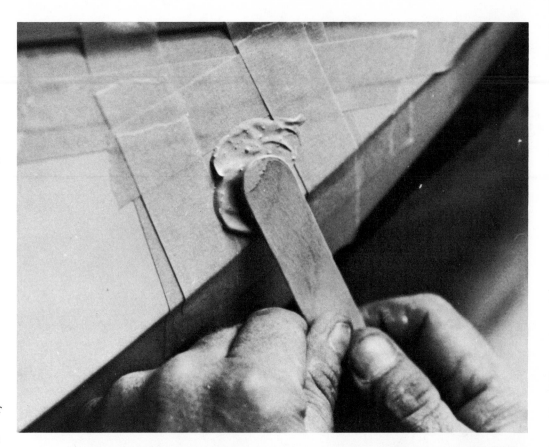

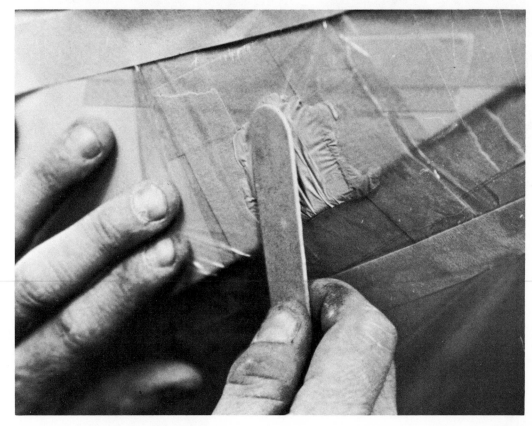

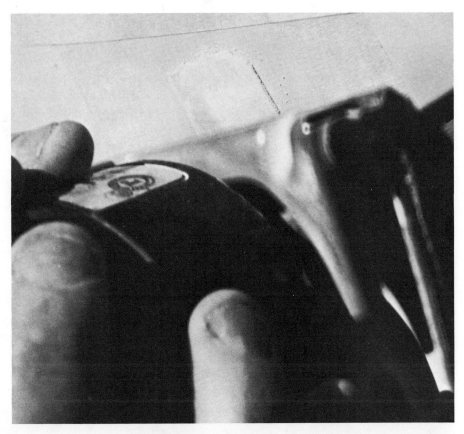

After the gel coat has cured, remove the plastic wrap and all but one layer of masking tape. Sand the repair down to the level of the hull surface. Use finer and finer sandpaper as you get close to the original surface. As a final treatment, use a 400-grit wet sandpaper, followed by a polishing compound. If your hull is colored, you'll want to make the repair the same color. Color-matching materials that enable you to make a very close match with the original color are available to mix with the gel coat before adding the catalyst.

If you need to repair a small hole in the hull, buy a patching kit containing the necessary materials. The first step is to clean out the hole and "scarf" or bevel the edges with a file or a disc sander. Bevel the hole from the inside only, so that the outside edge of the hole is smaller than the inside edge. If the hole is located so that you can work from the inside of the hull, do the scarfing as shown here. Make the edges of the hole clean and smooth so the patch will fit smoothly.

Use a dam on the outside of the hole to serve as a backup for the patch. This particular hole was on a shaped part of the hull, so a dam was formed from a small piece of aluminum sheet and taped in place with masking tape. Coat the surface of the aluminum dam with wax before taping it in place.

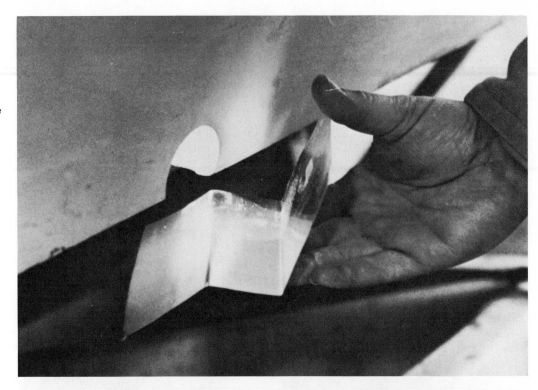

After the dam is in place, cut the fiber glass mat and fiber glass cloth to the size of the hole. This is easier to do when you can actually fit the piece into the hole for a trial fit. Remember that the patch is a build-up job with the smaller patch pieces against the outside of the hull. Working from the inside, apply gel coat to the hole. If the repair is in a vertical surface, use a mixture of half gel coat and half thickener to prevent sagging. The catalyst is added to this mixture.

Allow the gel coat to cure, which should take about an hour, before applying the patches. Then fit each patch into the hole and brush resin mixed with catalyst (follow the directions for mixing), soaking the patch. Brush thoroughly to remove any air bubbles. In order to match the original hull thickness, you will probably use two or more patches of fiber glass mat, followed by a final patch of fiber glass cloth. Allow the entire laminated surface to cure. You can help speed up the curing process by positioning a light bulb near the patch.

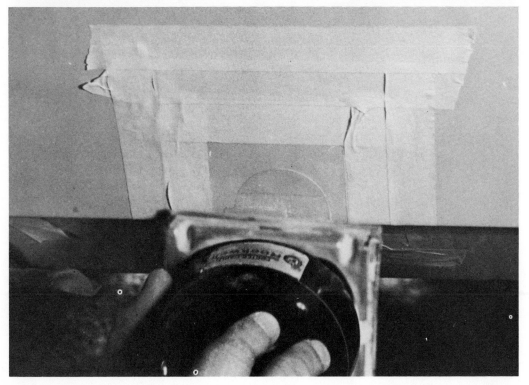

After the patch has cured, remove the aluminum dam from the exterior of the hull and sand the patch level with the hull's surface. Start with a 220-grit sandpaper; then go to a 400-grit paper. It's a good idea to put a layer of masking tape around the area before you start sanding to protect adjacent surfaces as you sand. The final sanding should be done by hand with wet garnet paper, followed by a polish with polishing compound.

If the hole is in a place which doesn't allow you to work from the inside of the hull, you'll have to do the entire patch job from the outside. The first step is to block the area out with protective paper and masking tape. Then use the disc sander or file to clean and "scarf" or bevel the edges of the hole as before, again making the outside hole area smaller than the inside hole area.

It is necessary to provide a back-up dam for the patch, which can be a bit tricky. Here a piece of waxed aluminum was rolled slightly and inserted through the hole. A hook made of a piece of coat hanger wire was inserted through two holes in the aluminum before insertion, and it was used to pull the aluminum into place over the hole. Once the dam is in place, brush catalyzed resin against the dam as a cement to hold the dam in place. Allow the resin to cure before proceeding; then remove the coat hanger. The easiest way is to use a wire cutter to clip the hanger near the surface of the aluminum.

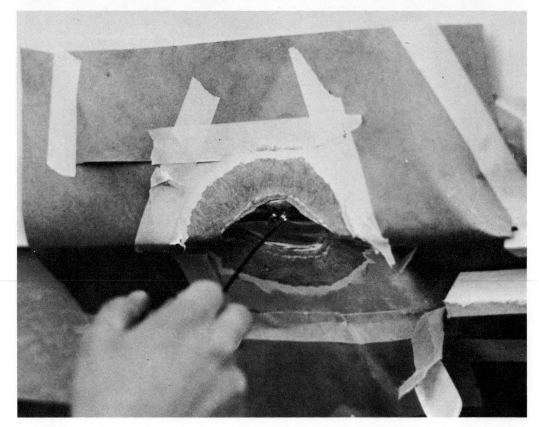

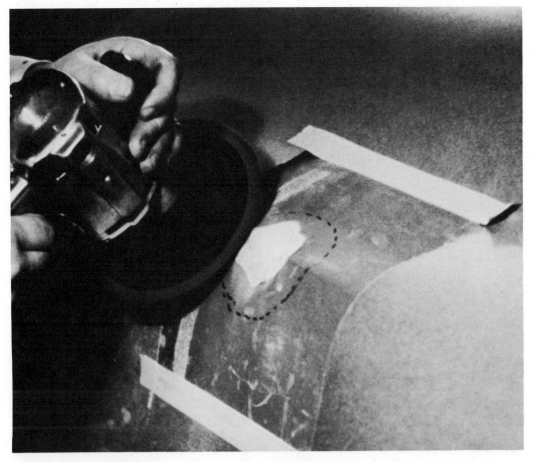

Build the laminated patch as before—but in reverse order. Apply the fiber glass cloth patch first, brushing it with catalyzed resin. Allow it to cure; then apply the fiber glass mat patches in the same manner. Finally, after the mats have cured, apply the thickened and catalyzed gel coat to the exterior. Build it up slightly above the original surface because the gel coat shrinks a little as it cures. After it has cured, sand the patch level with the hull's surface as described earlier, using a disc sander.

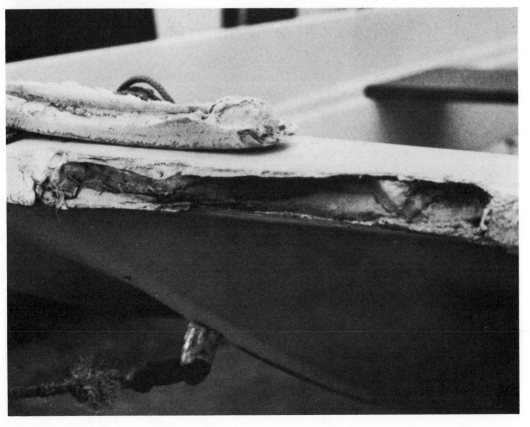

Some areas of a fiber glass hull may be fiber glass molded around foam material. Such is the case with the damaged bow of this boat, which apparently was traveling too fast when it hit a dock. To begin a repair of this area, remove the old foam and sand the edges of the damaged area clean; then bevel the edges.

Cut a piece of foam to fit into the patch. Use urethane foam, not polystyrene, since polyester resin will destroy a polystyrene foam. "Glue" the foam in place with a resin putty which you can buy ready-made or mix yourself by adding thickener and glass fibers to polyester resin. (One cup resin, 1/5 cup glass fibers, thickener as needed, plus a small amount of catalyst—2 percent by volume of the entire mixture.)

After the putty holding the foam in place has cured, use a disc sander to shape the foam to the proper contours. You can use more putty to help build up the contour, and then finish the job by applying fiber glass mat and fiber glass cloth with resin in alternating layers. After this has cured, apply the last coat of gel coat, covering it with plastic wrap until it cures. Finish the job as you did with the previously described patches.

Trailer Maintenance

Monetarily speaking, your boat trailer has a very heavy responsibility. It carries your entire boat and motor investment and puts a heavy strain on your automobile investment. This means that when you are towing your trailer, there is at least $6,000 of your money at stake — and the total is more likely closer to $10,000 or more.

Most of us are pretty careful of anything which is responsible for $10,000 of our hard-earned cash. But sometimes the trailer gets only stepchild treatment, with most of the tender loving care going to the boat and motor. Keep in mind that your boat spends 90 percent of its life on the trailer and should be evenly supported. Uneven support may cause warping or misshaping of the boat's hull. If you suspect that your trailer is too small, trade it in for a new and larger one. Such a trade could save you a lot of money in boat repairs.

A proper-fitting trailer should support the boat evenly, with the rollers under the structural members of the hull. Check to see that all of the rollers come in contact with the hull; if some do not, have them adjusted. Finally, make sure the boat is not too long for the trailer—it should not extend beyond the back end of the trailer.

The most important support point is under the stern of your boat because of the added weight of the motor. If the boat is not supported directly under the stern and extends beyond the end of the trailer, the weight of the stern could force a bend or "hook" in the hull.

Trailers are rated by manufacturers according to the total weight they can carry. Look for the Trailer Manufacturer's Association rating plate on the trailer which will specify the number of pounds the trailer is built to carry safely. When considering the weight of your boat and motor, remember to include the stuff you've put into the boat and add this to the weight of the boat and motor.

The beginning of the boating season is the best time to make a thorough inspection of your trailer and to do any necessary maintenance work. During the season you should have to do no more than keep the tires properly inflated and grease the bearings occasionally, particularly if they have been submerged in water.

PRESEASON CHECKUP
- *Trailer frame.* If there are nicks and scratches, or if rust spots have appeared, touch up these spots. Sand the damaged area down to bare metal; use paint in a spray can to rebuild the finish, first laying down a coat of metal primer, followed by two coats of finish coat. Automobile touch-up enamels are fine for this job, and they dry quickly.

   Sight along the frame to see that it isn't bent or sagging. Bending or sagging usually is a sign that your boat is too big for the trailer.
- *Tires.* Examine the tire treads and replace tires that are worn. Check for cuts and breaks in the side walls. These tires must carry a heavy weight—sometimes over rough roads—and weaknesses mean potential blowouts. Check the air pressure. Underinflation is the leading cause of premature tire wear. In fact, you should check the air pressure before each trip and get into the habit of visually

Every trailer is designed to carry a certain maximum load and should bear the Trailer Manufacturer's Association plate specifying the maximum carrying capacity. Look for this plate and, for safety reasons as well as for the protection of your equipment, do not exceed the limit. Remember this limit is the *total* safe weight of the load on the trailer, which includes the boat, and motor, and all the gear you have stowed in the boat.

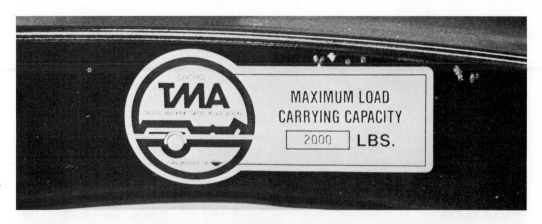

It is a good idea for all the drivers in the family to know how to handle a trailer. Set up flags like this on a big, empty parking lot and let each driver practice backing between them until each feels confident that he or she can handle the trailer.

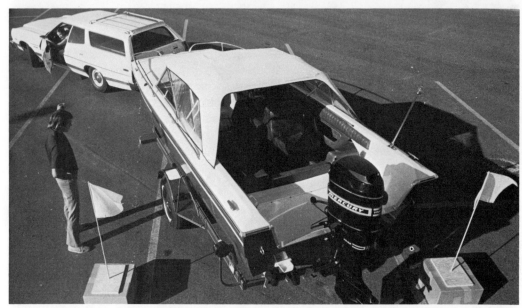

When launching a boat, it is best not to back a trailer into the water over its axles. Have someone signal as you back up, indicating when the trailer has reached the water's edge.

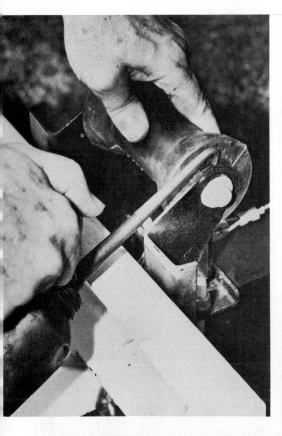

Far left:
During your spring maintenance check of the trailer, oil all of the rollers to make launching and retrieving of the boat easier.

Left:
Oil all of the working parts of the trailer winch. These parts are exposed to a lot of water and dirt during the boating season and can become difficult to work if not lubricated frequently.

Start the season off with the correct air pressure in your trailer tires, and make a habit of checking the pressure regularly. Low pressure causes serious tire wear and may affect the ride and handling of the trailer.

checking the tires every time you walk around the trailer. Low tires steal money from your pocket.

Check for bent wheels by jacking up the trailer frame and spinning each wheel and observing its rotation. Check for axle sag by laying a straightedge on top of the axle. If the axle sags when the boat is on the trailer, it is a good indication that the trailer is overloaded.

- *Springs.* Inspection may reveal a broken leaf in one of the springs or springs which have become fatigued and lost their springing ability. These are jobs for a mechanic. A more common ailment is a worn shackle bushing. A shackle is a bolt assembly which ties the spring to the frame. A rubber bushing surrounds each bolt and when these become worn, the springs become noisy and loose. You can pull the old bushings out with a pair of pliers and insert new ones.

  Lubricate the springs by squirting automotive grade motor oil so that it can work its way between the leaves.

- *Coupler.* Two vital links on all trailers are the coupler and the tilt hinge boat. Check these for wear, and see that they are tight on the trailer tongue. Look to see that all bolts around these are tight and that any welding is solid and free from cracks.

- *General lubrication.* Oil all moving parts—the winch, the coupler, and all rollers. If you have a swiveling nose wheel with a crank, oil all its moving parts.

- *Safety chains.* Never tow a trailer without connecting the safety chains between the trailer hitch and the trailer tongue. The recommended method of hitching the chains is to cross them under the tongue. The reason is that if the trailer coupler should come off the ball, the crossed chains will

support it and keep it off the road.

- *Wiring.* The electrical wiring of a trailer is exposed to the weather and subject to accidental breakage. The wires are small and are often positioned where anyone climbing on the trailer could break them without realizing what had happened. The connector between the power supply on the car and the trailer gets a lot of wear and weathering, too.

  At the beginning of the season examine all wiring for breaks and signs that the insulation has deteriorated. If cracks, even tiny ones, develop in the insulation, you have a potential short circuit.

  Rewiring a trailer usually isn't difficult. Buy spools of the correct wire size (your dealer has it, and any electrical supply house can match the wire) in the same colors used by the manufacturer. The existing wire will serve as your instruction sheet. Simply replace it.

- *Lights.* Remove the lenses from your trailer lights and clean the inside of each one. Rinse out any accumulation of dirt, and allow the unit to dry thoroughly. Replace burned out bulbs and replace the lens seals. Coat the contacts inside each light with grease or petroleum jelly to protect them from moisture.

- *Rollers.* You've already made sure that each roller is in contact with the hull and you've lubricated them. As you roll the boat off and on the first time in the season, observe to see that each roller is actually rolling. Some may bind and make launching and loading difficult. Replace them. If your trailer has bunks instead of rollers, replace these when they become worn.

- *Winch rope.* You might easily suffer serious injury if the winch cable on your trailer snaps as you are cranking the boat up during

If your trailer was noisier than it should have been last season, the reason might be worn shackle bushings on the springs. The shackle bushing is a rubber piece inserted over the bolts which hold the springs to the trailer. To inspect the bushings, use an automobile tire wrench to remove the bolts holding the shackle plate in place. Lift the shackle plate off and you'll be able to see the rubber bushings around the bolts. If they appear worn so that the bolt can move excessively in its housing, replace them. Pull the old bushings out with a pair of pliers; push new ones into place. Bushings can be purchased where you bought your trailer. Replace the shackle plate and the bolts.

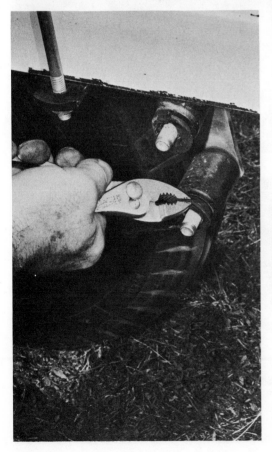

loading. In the beginning of the season, run out the entire cable and look for frays or broken strands. Don't take chances: if the cable is not in perfect condition, replace it. Remember, the only time the cable will break is under pressure—when you are hauling the boat out of the water. After snapping under tension, the cable flies for a moment and is a lethal weapon. When replacing the cable, get a sturdy one. Keep in mind that with all the gear in it, the boat weighs considerably more than it did on the showroom floor. The original cable may have been matched to the empty boat.

Another critical element of the launching/loading operation is the bow eye on the boat to which the winch cable is attached. Look it over to see that it hasn't become loose and isn't cracked or bent.

WHEEL BEARINGS

The wheel bearings on your trailer are its most critical part. They suffer because all too often you must back down a ramp so far that the trailer wheels are submerged. This is bad enough in fresh water and even worse in salt water. The water gets into the bearings, emulsifies the grease, and

Remove the cover from each light on the trailer and clean out any water or dirt which has accumulated inside. Be sure the cover fits tightly and that all screws are tight when you replace it. Check to see that all bulbs are operable, and replace any that are burned out.

If the light is working properly, coat the electrical connections inside the case with a film of heavy grease or petroleum jelly. This protects them from corrosion if water should get into the case.

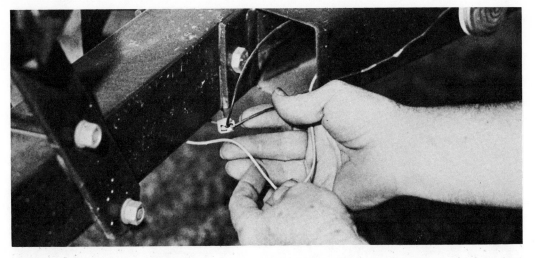

All electrical wires should be examined carefully in the beginning of each boating season. Look for broken wires and for frayed or cracked insulation on the wires. If the insulation shows signs of deterioration, replace the wire, since water may get to the wires and cause a short circuit.

causes it to lose its lubricating qualities. The next thing you know, you have a frozen or burned out bearing.

The most important time to repack the wheel bearings is when you put the trailer into winter storage. If there is water in the grease when you put the rig away, or if the grease has been emulsified, corrosion or pitting will take place in the bearings and bearing housings during the storage period.

Manufacturers recommend that you pack the bearings at least twice a year, but more frequently if the trailer wheels are often submerged. Tools needed for the job are a wrench, a screwdriver, a pair of pliers, plus a tube of grease (the label usually says wheel bearing grease, but the official specifications are Lubriplate Marine A or No. 70).

You should also have a jack for your trailer. The average automobile jack isn't safe or strong enough to use for hoisting a trailer. A small diamond-frame jack is better. Remember to block the trailer wheels securely when the rig is on the jack.

There are two kinds of wheel bearing installations. In the more common, you jack the trailer up, pull off the hub and protective dust cover, take the bearings from the housing, and clean out the old grease. Then you apply new grease and reassemble the unit. (See photographs.) In the second type, you attach a grease gun to the bearing assembly and pump grease into the area. If you have this second type, follow the manufacturer's directions.

INSPECTION CHECKLIST

Make a habit of walking around the trailer before each trip; use the following checklist to guide your inspection.

☐ Are all parts, nuts, and bolts tight?

☐ Are all moving parts lubricated?

☐ Are tires inflated to correct pressure?

☐ Have the wheel bearings been lubricated properly?

☐ Are all boat tie-downs properly secured?

☐ Are all lights operating properly?

☐ Is the trailer hitch tight?

☐ Are the safety chains secured?

☐ Are the trailer brakes operating properly?

☐ Is the motor tight on the boat transom?

☐ Does the motor have sufficient road clearance?

☐ Is any baggage or equipment carried in the boat tied down?

☐ Is baggage or equipment in the boat evenly distributed in the boat?

☐ Are gas tanks tightly closed? (The safest way to travel is with empty boat gas tanks; fill them when you get to the water.)

☐ Is the boat cover securely anchored so it will not tear off or flap in the wind?

This series of photos shows the easy and safe way to connect a trailer to the trailer hitch on your car. (1) Crank the trailer tongue up until it is slightly higher than the level of the ball on the car. (2) Grasp the tongue and move it forward over the ball. Reverse the crank and let the tongue down on the ball.
(3) Push the locking mechanism down tightly so that the trailer tongue is locked to the ball.
(4) Connect the safety chains between the trailer and the hitch. The best way is to cross the chains under the trailer tongue as shown in the picture. Then, if the tongue should come off the ball, the chain will support it until you can stop. Finally, connect the electrical plug from the trailer to the electrical plug from your car.

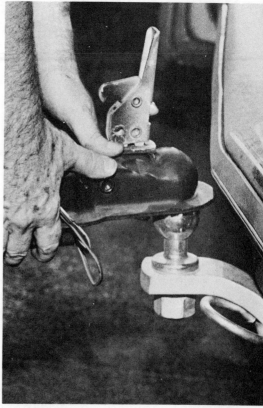

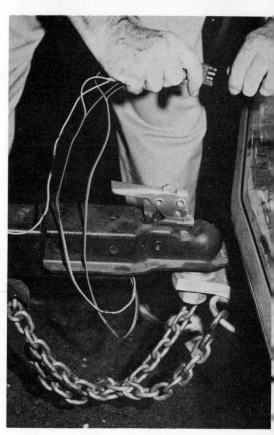

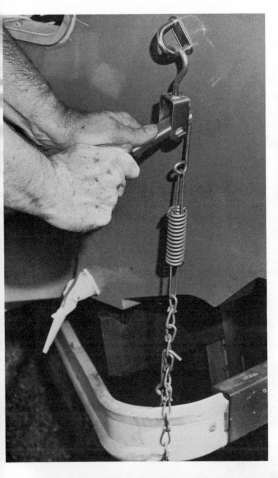

Before you move the trailer: (1) check to see that the tie-downs which hold the boat on the trailer are tightly fastened; (2) check to see that the canvas cover on the boat, if it has one, is secured in place and won't flap as you drive; and (3) be sure the motor is set for trailering.

Note: These photographs were taken of a trailer wheel and axle off a trailer and on a stand in order to make close-up pictures possible. To repack the wheel bearings on your trailer, jack the trailer up, using a good scissors or 3-point type jack (not the jack which comes with your car). Most automotive stores have these jacks which provide much safer support. In addition, put wheel blocks in front and back of the wheel you are not working on.

The wheel bearings on your trailer should be repacked with grease at the beginning of each boating season, regularly during the season—especially if you have backed the trailer into the water over its axle—and, most important of all, when you store the trailer for the winter. Follow these steps to prepare the trailer wheel to be repacked: (1) remove the hub cap; (2) remove the wheel by using an automotive lug wrench on the wheel nuts; (3) with the wheel off, use a screwdriver and a hammer to gently tap off the dust cover on the end of the trailer axle.

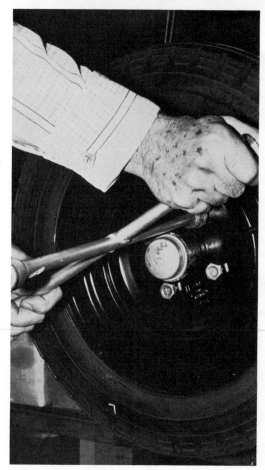

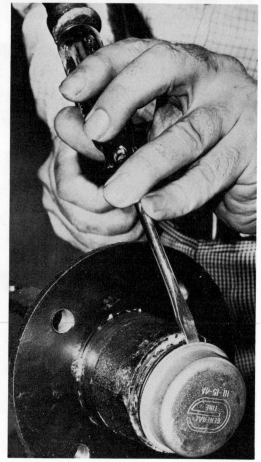

With the dust cover off the axle, straighten the arms of the cotter pin which were bent over to secure it in place; then use a pair of pliers and a hammer as shown to remove the cotter pin.

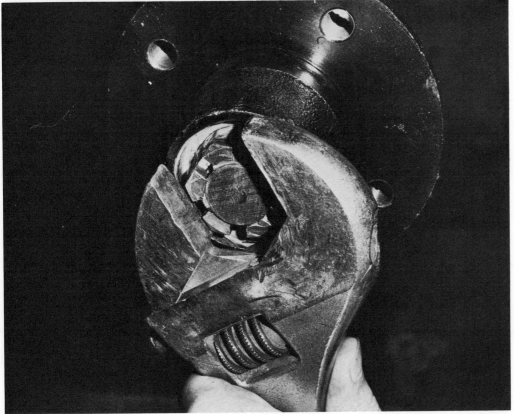

Using a wrench, loosen and remove the axle nut.

Reach into the housing with your fingers and remove the bearing.

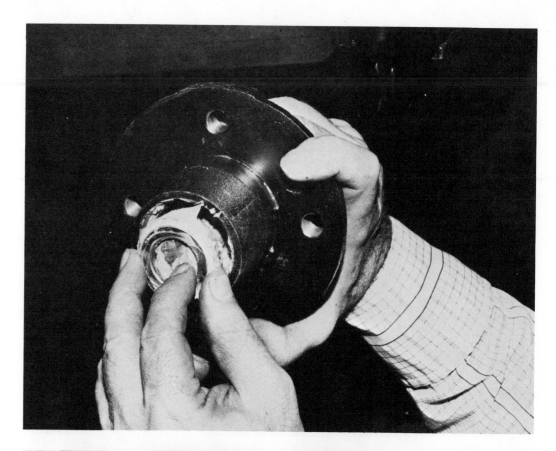

There are two bearings in each trailer wheel, an outside and an inside bearing. After removing the outside bearing with your fingers, remove the bearing housing from the axle. It should come off after a couple of sharp blows with the heel of your hand.

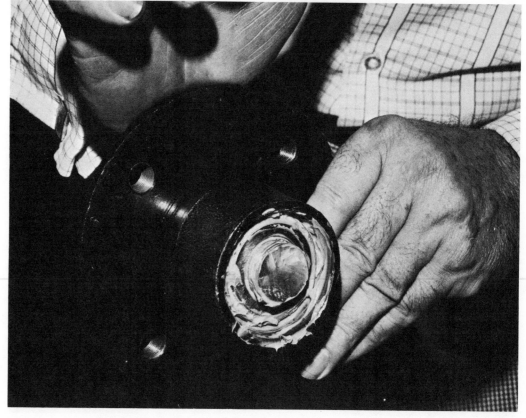

With the bearing housing off the axle, use a screwdriver to remove the bearing retainer which holds the inside bearing in place. Do this carefully so as not to damage the retainer. It should pry out easily.

Lift out the bearing.

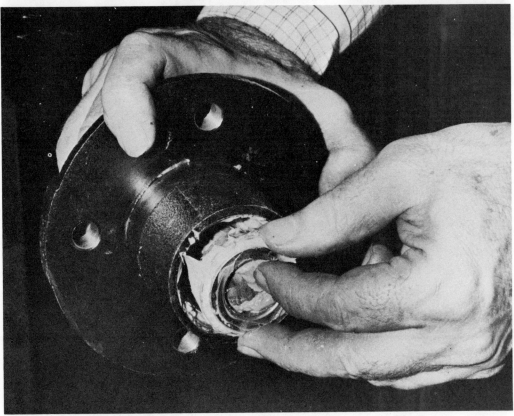

Clean the old grease from the housing and from the bearing, and apply a generous amount of new grease. Put the bearing back in place.

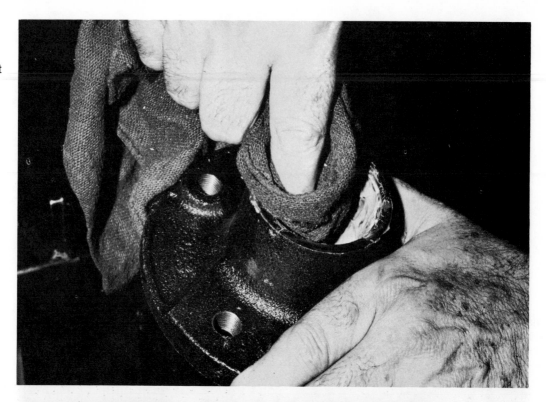

Put the bearing retainer back in place and tap it gently with a hammer to seat it.

After the inside bearing has been greased and installed, put the bearing housing back on the axle. It slips easily into place. Now clean both the housing and outside bearing of old grease, and apply new grease. Slip the bearing back into its original position. Thread the axle nut back on the axle and tighten it moderately with a wrench. Spin the wheel to be certain it turns easily. Now install a new cotter pin as shown, pushing it all the way into the hole in the axle. Use a pair of pliers to bend over the arms of the cotter pin. Finally, reinstall the dust cover. Put it in position; then gently tap it into its seat using a hammer and screwdriver. Put the wheel back on, replace the hub cap, and the job is done.

Safe and Sane Operation

Not including severe sunburn and grouchy in-laws, there are three things which can interrupt your fun afloat:

1. An equipment breakdown
2. Bad weather
3. An accident

If you follow the maintenance procedures in this book, you should improve your chances of avoiding equipment breakdowns. The vast majority have been shown to result from maintenance oversights.

Bad weather can in most cases be avoided. The wise boater learns to watch the weather and soon develops an instinct about it. But he also keeps a radio on board tuned to the weather band, and listens to weather reports each hour. He doesn't want to get caught out in a storm in case his weather instincts are wrong.

These are most basic weather rules in boating: 1) Check the weather before you leave the dock, and don't go out if you have doubts about it. 2) If you are out in a boat, head back to shore as soon as you receive a weather warning. High winds and high seas can put you in a tough situation.

You should know how to handle your boat in all kinds of weather. Take one of the boating courses offered by the Power Squadron or Coast Guard Auxiliary. Experts agree that the greatest prevention of boating mishaps is boating education. The more you know about your equipment and how to handle it, the less likely you are to get into trouble.

Every boat has different handling characteristics, and you should learn all there is to know about your boat—particularly how to handle it in rough water and high winds. There will be some storms you can't avoid, and when you get into one of these, you should know what to do.

To avoid accidents, know the rules of the road, stay alert, and use common sense. Try to anticipate dangerous situations. Equip each person in the boat with a personal floatation device—the new name for life jackets—and install a fire extinguisher in your boat, ready for trouble.

The pictures, captions, and charts in this chapter are a refresher course in operational safety. The situations are all familiar, and the charts don't present any information the average skipper has not seen before. But check them anyway. They, like the maintenance material here, may help you to have uninterrupted fun afloat.

Camping on the bank of a river is a great family sport, but when you turn the boat toward the bank, take it slow and easy. This is probably new water for you. Be careful with propellers in the shallow water, and watch for logs and old tree roots which often lurk just under the surface of the water.

Channel Buoy Guide

Entering port or going upstream

PORT SIDE   Color: Black odd numbers

Lighted

Can

Spar

Unlighted Bell

Unlighted Whistle

MID-CHANNEL   Color: Black & White no numbers

Lighted

Can

Spar

Nun

JUNCTION   Color: Red & Black

Lighted

Can

Spar

Nun

STARBOARD   Color: Red even numbers

Lighted

Spar

Nun

Unlighted Bell

Unlighted Whistle

Coastal Warning Display System

Whenever winds dangerous to navigation are forecast, the United States Weather Bureau displays coastal warning signals: RED and BLACK flags by day; RED and WHITE lights by night.

Warning: Skin Diver in Area.

Color: red with white diagonal stripe

DAY SIGNALS   NIGHT SIGNALS

 Small Craft Warning. Winds up to 30 miles an hour (33 knots) and/or sea conditions dangerous to small craft operations forecast for the area.

 Gale Warning. Winds from 39 to 54 miles an hour (34 to 48 knots) forecast for area.

 Whole Gale Warning. Winds from 55 to 73 miles an hour (48 to 63 knots) forecast for area.

 Hurricane Warning. Winds 74 miles an hour (64 knots) and above forecast for area.

Rules of the Road

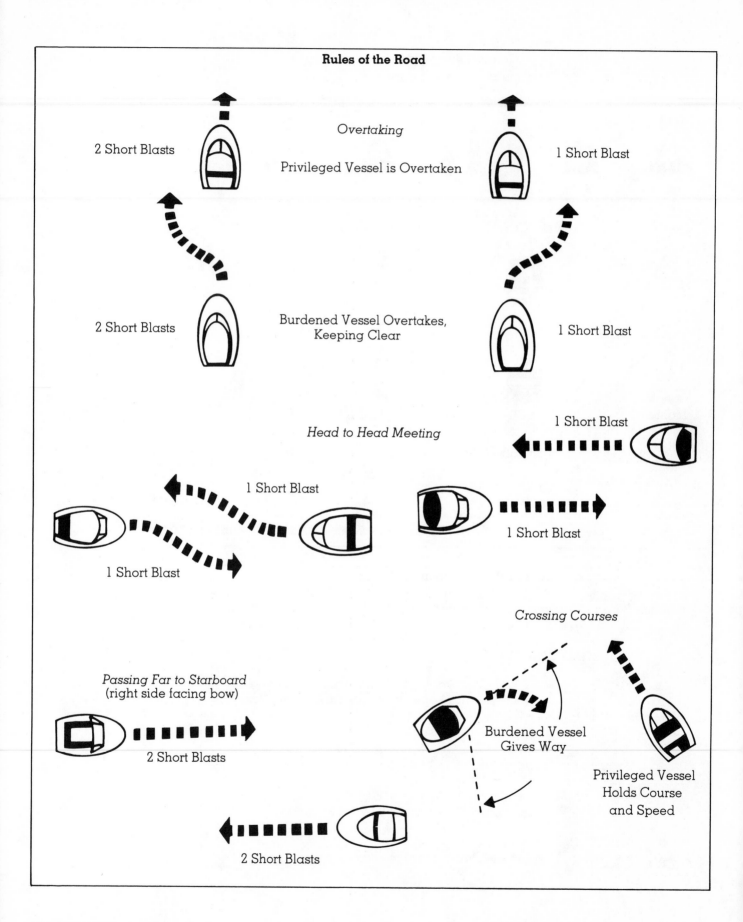

Overtaking

Privileged Vessel is Overtaken

2 Short Blasts

1 Short Blast

2 Short Blasts

Burdened Vessel Overtakes,
Keeping Clear

1 Short Blast

Head to Head Meeting

1 Short Blast

1 Short Blast

1 Short Blast

1 Short Blast

Crossing Courses

Passing Far to Starboard
(right side facing bow)

Burdened Vessel
Gives Way

2 Short Blasts

Privileged Vessel
Holds Course
and Speed

2 Short Blasts

Water skiing is the most popular sport connected with boating—next to fishing. Here is a group of skiers who know what they're doing. There is a safety lookout in the boat in addition to the driver, and both skiers are wearing personal floatation gear.

This family is headed for some trouble-free boating fun and they've brought all the safety devices they need, including a paddle and floatation equipment. But to make sure they won't need the paddle, they should make sure the clamps are tight on the transom. Even better, they should attach a safety chain so that if the motor should come off the boat, it won't be lost in the depths of the lake.

You can't blame this man for playing that good bite, but unless he's careful, he'll be in the water alongside his fish. Standing up in a boat is one of the major causes of boating accidents.

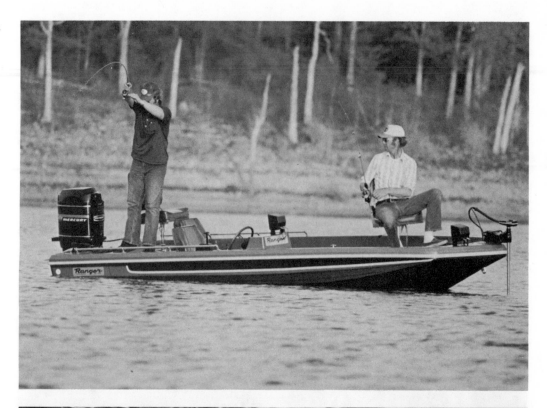

Skin and scuba diving are great fun, but divers need to be alert at all times. Other boats passing close by can't see the divers, and a spinning propeller can do terrible damage. Safety experts recommend that you mark your diving area with a buoy flying the "diver down" flag—a red flag with a diagonal white stripe.

This outboard is entering one of the locks on the upper Mississippi. Locking-through is simple, but you should know the procedure, just as you should know all the rules of the road.

This little marina tucked into a cove along the beautiful St. Croix River is almost hidden from the rest of the world. Safety problem here? Not really. Just a boat handling problem. When maneuvering your boat in confined places such as this, go slowly. Do not make any quick or sudden moves. Nobody loves the roaring "cowboy," especially near other boats.

The water is rough, but these fishermen are in a hurry to get out to where the big ones are biting. They would save a lot of fuel and have a smoother trip by throttling back a bit.

Wearing floatation jackets and carrying these floatation cushions, this pair is well-equipped for a safe and enjoyable outing.

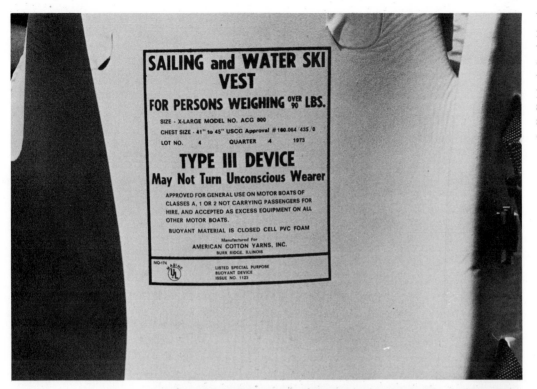

When you purchase floatation gear, check for the Coast Guard approval label. It not only tells you that the gear has passed Coast Guard standard tests but also sets safety limits for the equipment's use as well.

The wake of a passing boat can tip a fishing boat over—or kids can go overboard for a number of reasons. Every child in every boat should wear floatation gear—and a grin like this.

You can put on your own boat registration number in just a few minutes. Remember, you need a set on each side of the bow.

Index

surface preparation, 54
tools for painting, 54
vinyl cabin tops, 58
vinyl deck surfaces, 58
wood decks, 58
"Planing," 40
"Plowing," 39
Powerhead cleaning, 45, 47
Propeller
bent shaft, 8
inspection, 23, 48
making shaft watertight, 23, 34
replacing damaged propeller,
23, 24, 25
safety precautions, 25
selecting new propeller, 23, 35
smoothing rough edges, 37, 38
spare propellers, 23

R

Rating plate
boat, 36
trailer, 71, 72
Record keeping, 7
Rules of the road, 88
Rust preventives, 44, 45

S

Safe boat operation, 86
Saltwater
flushing after use in, 44, 46
in trailer bearings, 76
Scuba diving, 90
Signals, 87

Skin diving, 90
Spare parts list, 11
Spark plugs
disconnection of cables, 48
gap adjustment, 17, 18
gapping tool, 17
gasket, 19
inspection, 16
removal, 16, 17
surface gap type, 17
torque wrench, 19, 20
wrench for removal, 17
"Squatting," 39
Stabilizer, gasoline, 47
Storage
at dealer, 14
in driveway, 14
of motor, 45

T

Tachometer, 36, 38
Throttle settings, 40
Tilt angle adjustment, 38
Tires, trailer, 71
Tool kit, basic, 11
Tools, 10
Trailer
coupler, 74
frame, 71
hitch, 78
inspection, 71, 77, 79
lights, 74, 76
lubrication, 74
maintenance, 71, 73

rollers, 71, 73, 74
safety chains, 74
springs, 74
tires, 71, 73
wheel bearings, 76
how to repack, 80
when to repack, 77
types of bearings, 77
wheels, treatment after
submersion, 77
winch cable, 73, 74, 75, 76
wiring 74, 77
worn shackle bushings, 74, 75
Trailer Manufacturers'
Association, 71, 72
Trim tab adjustment, 38
replacement, 35
Trolling, 37, 40
Trolling motors, 40
Troubleshooting chart, 40, 41
Tune-up, motor, 33, 34, 35

U

U.S. Power Squadron, 86

W

Water intake ports, 21, 44
Water pump, 8, 41
drainage, 44
Water skiing, 89
Weather, 86
Wheel bearings. See Trailer
Wiring, boat, 34
Wood hull repairs, 60